# WAKE UP
## REFLECTIONS FOR SPIRITUAL AWAKENING
*The Essence of Yoga and Vedanta*

by Yogi Shanti Desai
www.yogishantidesai.com

Editing by Edward Glazier PhD
Typesetting and Book Cover by Gudjon Bergmann

# DEDICATION

To all the ancient masters

.

# CONTENTS

# ACKNOWLEDGMENTS

I want to thank Dr. Edward Glazier for editing this book. Ed has been studying with me and has been in touch with me for last 36 years. I also want to thank Gudjon Bergmann for typesetting and organizing this book. Gudjon is a good friend and student of mine since 1998. We trained 60 yoga teachers together at his yoga studio in Iceland from 2001 to 2006.

# EDITOR'S NOTE

This book was edited by a student who has read Shanti's books and correspondence with deep interest since 1981. Shanti has a direct style that brings readers quickly to essential meaning. The editor merely attempted to allow the author's style, lifetime of dedication to yoga, and basic message to shine forth.

.

# INTRODUCTION

I was driven to search for truth and have been practicing yoga from early childhood. This search continued as an undercurrent during my studies and years of employment. I graduated with a master's degree in chemistry from Drexel University and worked in the industry for eight years. But my heart was not in the profession. Spiritual undercurrents lead me to retire from worldly pursuits and dedicate more time to explore inward. Although I have been teaching since 1968 and retired to teach yoga full-time in January 1972, my own yoga practice and exploration of truth is a personal priority.

I studied scriptures and the teaching of masters and followed them literally. I wrote three books between 1976 and 1981 as text books for holistic yoga, hatha yoga and meditation for students. These were based on scriptures, inner research and teaching experience. I was not happy with the dogmatic approach of many masters. They made yoga inaccessible for the average person. They exaggerated concepts of celibacy, austerity, Guru, and mysteries of spiritual practices.

I questioned everything and met authorities and popular Gurus. They did not satisfy my hunger for knowledge. I relied on my practices, experiences and intuition. I wrote more books as I evolved. I communicated the ancient teachings in a concise and contemporary way as statements (Sutras). When I came across research findings from quantum physics, it answered many of my questions. It gave scientific validation to the teachings of ancient masters. One should complement faith with a scientific approach and direct understanding. This gives personal conviction.

I considered life as a school and experimented and explored. Teaching group classes and especially private classes, interacting with spiritual masters, and travelling gave me knowledge of human psychology and cultivated spiritual maturity. I learned much by running a yoga center in Ocean City, New Jersey for 39 years (1974-2013) and a yoga ashram in Glassboro, New Jersey for 8 years (1977-1985). I found that students have desire to become disciples and follow instead of taking charge of their lives. I also had lots of interaction with people oriented to health and spirituality while running Prasad health food store and restaurant for 19 years (1981-2000).

I was impressed in past years by several revolutionary spiritual masters. I listened to their lectures and tried to reach them for Satsang (discussion of Truth). Most of them were wrapped up in building their following and building their own organizations and had no time. I found that most of their talk was intellectual and not from personal practice. Other teachers were threatened, fearing their students would leave if I awakened them to the truth. I came to the same conclusion the ancient masters had taught: "Be thy own lamp." This relieved me of the burdens of searching outside. My joy comes from awakening people who are ready to wake up.

Travelling into various countries and cultures over the years gave me deeper understanding of human mind. I trained about 10 groups of yoga teachers at the studios of students in Iceland. This occurred during 12 visits (between 1997 and 2007). I have noticed that human nature remains the same regardless of prosperity, education environment, or country. Human nature is expressed differently with advances in technology and communication, but in general, technological advancement and economic freedom have not benefitted those without spiritual wisdom.

My wife and I visited India during January and February of 2017. We made spiritual contacts and taught yoga and meditation to various groups. We visited famous temples, ashrams, charitable organizations, historical places and popular tourist attractions.

We had toured most of India in 1974 with six yoga students. We had travelled from Rishikesh in the north to Kanyakumari at the southern tip of India and covered all tourist attractions along the way. It was a rugged trip on a mini-bus with two drivers and a guide. We travelled day and night to the most remote places, ashrams, and temples, eating and sleeping wherever we stopped. It was beautiful India with natural beauty and without invasion of commercial activities. We noticed changes in all phases of life over the subsequent visits.

After 43 years, we noticed exponential changes in all areas of life. Blind faith, dogmas and rituals are destroying spirituality. Commercialism has taken over and has influenced lifestyle of masses. Spiritual places have turned into commercial businesses where competition and gimmicks misguide masses. People have become more materialistic and are running blindly.

Birthplace of spiritual heritage is degraded. Spiritual masters build schools and dormitories, providing living and eating facilities from public donations. But hardly any teachers or students utilize them. Temples collect millions of dollars as donations but temples have become ruins. Many temples lack toilet facilities for millions of devotees. They charge people admission to get Darshan (vision) of deity after standing for hours in narrow congested lines and being pushed by the crowd. Free admission requires half day of standing in lines. Image of deity is in the inner dark corner and you do not get a chance to view it or meditate more than a few seconds. Vendors and beggars line up at the entrance gate. Priests and workers at the temple come after you to get donations. Prasad (offering of food) is sold. Masses of people jam up spiritual places. Hotels, restaurants and shops thrive on tourists. Devotees follow blindly. They are looking for miracles and follow harsh austerities. Their lives become more miserable but they do not see it. They do not want to hear or change.

Our beautiful hometown had no electricity, running water or paved roads. There was a beautiful lake and Shiva temple on the bank of the lake. Everyone knew each other. There was poverty, yet love and contentment. Now it is crowded with people, vehicles, buildings, shops, cattle, vendors and pollution. Even sidewalks are taken over by vendors and small businesses. There is no room to walk. The lake is dry and blocked by commercial businesses. Everyone is walking with cell phones.

Pavagadha Mountain is located four miles from our hometown. It was a place of beauty with greenery, lakes, valleys, wildlife and many steps to Kali temple on the mountaintop. We used to climb rugged steps, going through the woods and seeing wild plants and animals, bathing in lakes and getting panoramic view of villages in the valley. These days, commercial vehicles crowd the halfway point and a ropeway takes you to the top. Entire passage is jammed up with shops and restaurants. We experienced similar story with the other tourist attractions and holy places we visited.

I asked questions to the devotees and guides to better understand their practices and austerities, and the significance of symbolic deities. They do not know and have lost curiosity to explore. Most people and groups liked my teachings wherever I taught. They liked my revolutionary approach to life. I awakened them to think and question instead of following the trend. They asked me to write a book in Gujarati for their benefit. I decided to write this book in simple English, so that someone can translate it later. Basic teachings can awaken anyone at any age and any culture. I have been revolutionary in my thinking and want to awaken masses from mesmerizing environment and corruptions.

This book has three parts:

Part 1: The first part provides guidance to be able to think clearly and gain clarity needed to find direction and achieve goals in life. It shares my views on the meaning of waking up and living in the present. Please read this prior to the reflections provided later in the book because these reflections touch all areas of life. All the reflections touch upon "waking up" in various ways.

Part 2: While part 1 appeals to our mind, part 2 moves us from thinking to meditation and intuition. Again, waking up is not something to be understood but rather experienced. It is my hope that these first two sections will help you read the reflections and experience them – not just think about it. This part provides a chart that depicts who we are, the journey of life and the direction for meditation. It also provides affirmations to help reprogram the mind to wake up from old conditioning and illusions. The affirmations should be read on a regular basis.

Part 3: Use part 3 for daily reading and inspiration. Read one or two reflections slowly, contemplate and apply in daily life.

This book is the simplified essence of my previous thirteen books. It is simplified so that any person in any culture and at any stage of life can understand and apply in their life. It is suitable for skeptics, believers, and lay persons. The book deals directly with basic issues of life and provides logical and practical guidance. It teaches the essential message of the masters and scriptures in a contemporary way. Read and reread. Think, question and apply. Use simplified meditation and affirmations, which can be applied in daily life.

Spiritual practices are not for attaining anything or competition but for removing imaginary burdens. One does not need to torture body or mind, but rather make friendship with them. One should undo instead of doing. You do not have to give up anything with force, it drops away effortlessly. Life is a school. Accept it, accept yourself and flow with life. For more details on ancient philosophy, please refer to my previous thirteen books.

Yogi Shanti Desai, 2017
*www.yogishantidesai.com*

# PART 1: THE PROCESS OF WAKING UP

## 1. WAKE UP

The purpose of this book is to awaken people to think and choose proper direction in life. We are under the influence of cosmic illusion (Maya). Because of the influence of Maya, we get lost in survival, pleasure, power and greed. We are in a dream state and do not know it until we wake up. Waking up means knowing our true essence as immortal Self (Atman). One cannot see the earth moving because all objects around it are moving simultaneously and we do not have reference point to see it. If one goes in space beyond gravity, one can see the movement. Other way to see the movement of earth is by being aware of the movement of surrounding planets. In the same way we can see the dream to be unreal by waking up or being aware of changing reality around us.

From the day we are born, our education and media systems teach us how the world is. They have been beaming information to us, influencing our perception of how things are and how one should be. We go to school, get a job, pay bills and think this is how it is. The power of the popular media relies upon us to be asleep and unaware about the true nature of reality.

In fact, the root of our being is pure Consciousness, from which all things are projected. If our own pure Consciousness is at the root of all things, then who but us defines how things should be? We can project our own reality. We have put the power outside of ourselves when everything we need lies within us. We have set definitions and limitations on ourselves by perceiving that 'we

6

have to do this' or 'we have to do that'. By living in this manner we are unable to take advantage of all the universe has to give us.

Many tragedies in life or loss of dear things are blessings in disguise. They make us think of the purpose of life. But the impulse dies quickly. This is called cemetery renunciation (Smashan vairagya). We see the death of others, which reminds us of our own mortality. This awakening does not last because of influence of Maya. We may repeat the same habits and lifestyle even if we are granted several hundred years to live. We can wake up a sleeping person but cannot wake up one who pretends to be awake. One has to remain awake continuously to transform life.

The process of waking up is painful. One evolves gradually. First one has to slow down and search honestly. Then one recognizes his or her own faults. One's ego will resist admitting faults. But the goal of understanding the Self will lead to a search for the cause and solution. One follows the right path, but old conditioning leads to rebellion. One does not see visible progress and loses patience. When one succeeds with earnest desire and by keeping an undercurrent of desire for liberation, willingness to sacrifice attachments and pleasures becomes easier to wake up. One becomes empty of expectations and the true journey toward awakening begins.

Waking up requires introspection and choosing direction towards Self instead of being slave to the world. Permanent waking up is liberation from transmigration and miseries (Moksha).

People are mesmerized by hypnotizing influence of greedy leaders, preachers, media and commercials. Technology can provide comforts and information to improve life. But it produces many distractions. Technological gadgets have made people dependent, like slaves and addicts. They have lost capacity to communicate and think creatively. These gadgets have produced restlessness among the masses. Most people complain of not having enough time and are discontented. As technology has evolved, it has provided comforts at the cost of peace of mind. It has shrunk consciousness of people and their capacity for compassion.

Swamis and Gurus have made spiritual path secretive, mysterious and unattainable for the average person. Other leaders claim miracles and instant Samadhi or awakening.

One Yogi and Swami from India introduced millions of people to the practice of yoga and Ayurvedic remedies. His teaching became popular due to his claim that it could cure illnesses, including incurable diseases such as Alzheimer's and rare cancers. This claim was supported by various patients who came on TV commercials claiming to be healed in a short time. Masses of people were mesmerized by the so-called miracles. People who are desperate support such quacks. The movement spread like wildfire. Many people became involved. Some became teachers and volunteers, supporting the movement for recognition or personal gain. Hardly anyone questioned or challenged the Swami or did anything to promote scientific aspects of yoga. It encouraged masses of people to practice yoga in large crowds as physical exercises. This happened in most of the villages in India. Many practitioners got hurt without proper personal guidance and by giving up their medications prematurely in hope of miracles. The Swami became one of the ten richest men in India by manufacturing and selling Ayurvedic products through retail stores. Many people joined his franchise of stores as a business venture. Another famous Guru started another line of Ayurvedic products to compete with him. Awakening people is a good thing but misleading them for personal gain is a spiritual crime.

Commercial leaders have created fancy names for straightforward yoga practices, such as Sudarshan kriya, yoga nidra, transcendental meditation, Sahaj Samadhi, kundalini, chakras and others. Yoga teachers have created yoga brand names after their own name, for certain sequences of positions. They have created rope yoga, block yoga, partner yoga, hammock yoga, paddleboard yoga, chair yoga and hot yoga to attract clients. Healers and martial artists have exploited their training by giving grades and certifications to students to make money. Today, yoga teachers often rely on professional certifications rather than their own spiritual growth and insight to guide students.

Most spiritual leaders and writers stimulate people's minds and emotions by providing illusion of wealth or instant success. The resulting impulse to practice dies quickly and people do not open their hearts to take responsibility to transform their lives. Many translations and interpretation of scriptures have been intellectual, literal or dogmatic. Many scholars distort the essential meaning of scriptures.

Wake up from relying on external authorities and their propaganda. You become a victim only if you seek miracles or a quick fix. How can a spiritual master awaken you to the spiritual path, if he himself is running after wealth, fame and power?

## 2. THINK CLEARLY

Most people follow blindly and belong to some religion or dogma of upbringing without thinking. They follow rituals and austerities without questioning. People look for answers from external authorities. They get converted and cover up their insecurity. During our recent trip to India, we noticed that masses of people were crowding the temples. They spend lots of money on extravagant weddings and building fancy houses. But they also overload scooters and rickshaws with many passengers. They walk with cell phones and wait in line for junk food at dirty street vendors. They are in their own world of hypnotic spell but think they are in heaven. Streets are crowded with vehicles without regulations, with horns blowing all the time. Pollution is taken for granted.

Masses of people crowd the temples with offerings of fruits and flowers to deities to gain prosperity. They follow unscientific austerities, torturing their body for some future gain. New spiritual leaders pop up all the time and thousands of disciples join them instantaneously. Disciples are desperate and become victims of con artists. People are running and have no time to think or rest. Spiritual journey begins only when you have time to settle down and think for yourself. Spiritual path is a personal and lonely path. Hanging on to others is like holding on to a balloon to float in the sky. Balloon can leak or pop and you crash to the ground. One needs to keep feet on the ground and heart in heaven.

No one can eat for you or take away your pain. They can only assist or guide you. Hanging on to any external authorities only makes you dependent like crutches. An absentee Guru, dead Guru or scriptures cannot help you in times of need. They cannot answer your questions or resolve your confusion. One needs a live Guru who can guide you. A lighted candle has potential to light many candles. A picture of a candle cannot. You should consider Guru as your mentor to inspire and guide you. We should not be attached to the finger of the Master, but rather follow the direction it is pointing.

Spiritual evolution begins only when you think clearly and inde-pendently. First empty the mind of all thoughts, beliefs and prejudices. An open and quiet mind can be cultivated more easily than a previously programmed mind. I have been able to teach yoga and meditation to new students more easily than those who are already programmed by previous training and certificates with various brand names.

Question your birth religion. Religious beliefs are introduced from birth and are taken for granted. A child can be switched at birth and will believe the religion of upbringing instead of religion of real parents. Reinvent your birth religion with understanding and apply it with fresh awareness instead of following blindly. First question and get logical answer, then practice and apply. Hearing (Sruti), logical analysis (Yukti) and personal experience (Anubhuti) are three recommended steps. The lives of persons who follow this direction are transformed permanently.

One should read original scriptures in their original language instead reading the interpretations of scholars. One should listen to the original master who has found Self. This is called Shravana. One should analyze and contemplate. This is called Manan. Then take it deeper into meditation. This is called Nididhyas. This process will transform life.

Spiritual path is suitable only for brave persons who take responsibility and address the challenges of life. As one increasingly relies on Self, one awakens inner strength. Being alone with the Self removes loneliness. One maintains equilibrium in crowds or seclusion.

## 3. THINK OUT OF THE BOX

One has to be reborn like a bird. A bird's first birth is as an egg. Its second birth occurs upon hatching out of the egg. We have to hatch out of the egg of conditioning and cultivate intuition. This gives direct wisdom to flow with life.

A little practice with understanding is superior to intense mechanical practice. Meditation is superior to knowledge. Direct experience in meditation dissolves all doubts and liberates.

Thinking outside the box gives you freedom to control your life.

Only when we wake up to the fact that we have been manipulated, can we begin to create reality for ourselves and step outside the box of our current perceptions and definitions of reality. From birth we are taught by our parents, who often follow what their parents taught them.

We are the co-creator of our destiny. We have infinite potential. Our perceptions and conditioning limit our potential. What we project manifests in our life. One has to be able to think and visualize without boundaries of the known. There is hypothesis before research. Projection and visualization are the starting point of transformation. Science fiction of the past has become reality today. Quantum physicists discovered that physical atoms are vortices of energy that are constantly vibrating. So every material structure in the Universe including you and me radiates a unique energy signature.

Everyone is connected, like waves are connected to the ocean. This realization removes illusion of separate existence. We work collectively and utilize universal energy for recharging.

It is better to know how to utilize knowledge with wisdom than simply accumulate information. Food is valuable only if you can digest it so that is gives you energy. A fancy smart phone is only valuable if you have the skill to use it. If you try to gain knowledge only by following external authorities, it may be confusing and dangerous. It would be as if you acquired several medications for various problems and got mixed up about them. You can derive more benefits from simple yoga with proper understanding. You can design proper routine to suit your age and physical condition instead of persisting with a lengthy mechanical routine. A long fast without understanding can harm you, while a short fast can be highly beneficial if you understand the process. If you understand the process and benefits of meditation, you can practice efficiently and use it to enrich your life. Forcing your mind with harsh disciplines will only frustrate you.

While in India in 2017, we visited health centers and spent a few days to get cleansing and rejuvenation. There are health centers, naturopathic clinics and health spas catering to wealthy people. But these are businesses, and owners are using commercial gimmicks to attract more clients.

I taught yoga and meditation to various groups in India. Yoga teachers are certified just as they are now in the United States. But just like in the U.S. they do not know real yoga. Exercise routines are accepted as yoga. I always ask simple questions out of curiosity to authorities in their fields, just like I ask my professional yoga clients. Most of them are lost. They only recite what they have learned. Instead of thinking, questioning, and learning, they get preoccupied with getting certification to teach and lose capacity to think outside the box.

I have donated my books to various ashrams and colleges over the years. They are gone whenever I visit the next time. I have also given my books to many students and groups. People seem to be extremely interested. Some have said they were going to e-mail me for further guidance, but I never heard from them again. Many organizations have resisted my teachings for fear of losing their dogmas. Spiritual leaders have been threatened by my revolutionary teachings, fearing they will lose control over their followers if I awaken them.

We are victims of our mind. We think in a linear direction like a horse with blinders. We should use mind like a helicopter instead of like a car. A car can only travel in linear direction while helicopters have greater freedom. We have potential to project the mind. We can determine our destiny.

## 4. QUANTUM LEAP

The basic teaching of Vedanta is validated by quantum physics. There is only one consciousness (Brahman). Everything else is empty space with electromagnetic energy. Brahman is cosmic ocean while all living creatures are like waves. Interaction of energy gives the illusion of names and forms. Everyone and everything is interconnected.

We are the co-creator of our destiny and can make a quantum leap. Quantum leap in science means an electron jumps from one orbit to another orbit. This is an abrupt change from one energy level to another with the loss or gain of a quantum of energy. This is a sudden and significant change.

In the human realm, quantum leap is the process by which a person can envision and attain some desired result or state of being that is clearly very different from the existing situation. What makes this possible is that, like a quantum particle, a person has the ability to exhibit quantum behavior.

Visualization, intention, intensity and affirmation are needed. One can lose weight or improve athletic performance and business or spiritual success by visualizing and believing it has already been achieved.

Relax, clear the mind, affirm and envision being healthy, wealthy or wise and sustain that experience until it registers in the unconscious mind. Envision some way of making a connection with unconscious mind, through a bridge, a door or a window. Cultivate ability to form a strong intention, to concentrate, and stay focused while being simultaneously relaxed and open-minded. This reprogramming will change the behavior pattern effortlessly until success is achieved.

With inner depth of understanding, intention and intensity, we have the potential to make a quantum leap toward liberation. Electrons travel in their normal orbit, but once in a while they jump to higher orbits when there is a burst of higher energy. Most people follow traditional ways, going through austerities and rituals. They get lost in the means and forget the goal. A quantum leap is the direct approach to liberation.

If one sets Self-Realization as the goal with urgency and intensity, one can bypass many unnecessary rituals and austerities. Our essential nature is perfection and bliss. In reality, we do not need any effort to attain what we really are. We only need to remove veils of ignorance and realize it. We are in the cosmic dream of Maya and need to wake up and become free. Dreams become unreal upon waking up. We can experience our true essence as permanent reality and world as impermanent projection upon it. A flashlight removes the darkness of ages. Waking up spiritually removes the darkness of ignorance in the same way. We can play our role in the world as an actor without attachments.

Consciousness is trapped in the gross, astral and causal bodies. Our original state of consciousness is Atman. Evolution takes us back to Atman and Self-Realization. This is called step-by-step process (Kramik). However, with intensity, urgency and focused attention, evolution can be quickened when seekers make a quantum leap in understanding and realization. This can be called direct process (Akramik).

13

One can reach the top floor of a skyscraper building by walking up steps, taking escalator or taking an elevator. Quantum leap is like taking an elevator.

We are programmed and hypnotized by body, senses, mind, intellect and I-Consciousness. We do not accept our full potential. Due to Maya, we believe that we are bound. We can remove darkness of cosmic illusion (Maya) with a spark of realization.

Yoga positions, breathing techniques, dietary disciplines, meditation techniques and austerities are only the means. The means preoccupy people and they forget the goal.

We live in a society of constant change and instant gratification. There is a lack of patience. It is easy to get lost. People need the spark of experience. After the experience they can use all the means necessary without imposition or force.

The process involves removing old conditioning, emptying the mind, and opening up to infinite potential. Nothing is impossible.

Try to do nothing and expect nothing, without goals or desires. Be empty. Enjoy aloneness of Self. It will reveal bliss, knowledge and guidance. It will provide fulfillment that will remove temptations of the world.

Let go of all burdens and become still. Just like electricity returns to its source, return to the source (Atman) effortlessly.

## 5. EVALUATION AND INTROSPECTION

Evaluation and introspection are required if you want to succeed in life. Without them there will be no direction or motivation. A businessman has to evaluate his assets and liabilities. He focuses on net profit instead of gross income. He sets direction for efficiency and success. Running several businesses is not a sign of success. Generating maximum profit within a short time and minimal effort is a sign of success.

Success in spiritual life requires evaluation and introspection. Financial success is only a means. One should be willing to sacrifice financial gain for moral living, good health, and peace of mind. One should not waste time trying to look good or impress others. One should earn spare time and seek out friends and environments that promote the spiritual journey. One maintains awareness of this goal and resets priorities to address changing situations, utilizing life for personal growth.

It is helpful to consider the following questions:

- How much time and energy do I direct to my true Self? How much energy do I waste trying to please the world?
- Am I utilizing the world and situations efficiently or am I slave to the world and my senses?
- Am I living to work or working to live? Am I working efficiently to survive and allowing time for personal growth and to enjoy life and relationships with others who support our primary goal?
- Am I in charge of my life or a slave to people and situations?
- Am I enjoying life here and now or waiting for perfect situations in future to find happiness?
- Do I talk to communicate and spread joy or gossip and waste energy and disturb the peace of others?
- Do I love unconditionally or am I attached to people and situations?
- Am I eating to live or living to eat?
- Do I take responsibility for my life or blame others for my problems?
- Is my life controlled by compulsive behaviors such as eating and shopping or do I choose carefully and make wise choices?
- Am I short-sighted or visionary?
- Do conflicts disturb me or does personal duty (Dharma) guide my life?
- Do I find conflicts among material, social, religious and spiritual life or do I utilize them to spiritualize my total life?
- Do I use my mundane duties and pursuits as means for spiritual evolution with a smiling face (Tapas), or am I using spiritual activities as an escape and to build ego?
- Are my wishes, hopes, and ambitions short-lasting impulses or do I put my desires into action without procrastination?
- Are my thoughts, speech and actions synchronized, or do I find conflicts and seek escape?

- Does my life revolve around cycles of indulgence, guilt, and suppression or do I enjoy a balanced life?
- Am I looking for a temporary relief or permanent cure?

Look over the last five years of your life. If you do not change the speed or direction your life is taking, where will you be five years from now? How many more years do you expect to live with a sound body and mind? What guarantee is there of tomorrow? Wake up and create urgency for Self-Realization. Remove illusions, set priorities and learn to live in the moment with awareness. Do you want to be free? Who is binding you? Realize that you are free here and now. There is nothing to do, nowhere to go and nothing to attain.

Wake up and realize you are like a lion lost in a flock of sheep. You are a prince or princess who has been kidnapped by thieves.

## 6. HUMAN LIFE IS A PRECIOUS GIFT

Humans evolved from simple forms of life over billions of years. Evolution involves increasing complexity, diversity, organization and complexity. The human body is the climax of evolution. It has self-reflective consciousness and the potential for liberation.

Minerals contain gross matter. Plants contain matter and Prana. Animals possess matter, prana and mind. Humans possess the two additional faculties of intellect and I-Consciousness. Intellect allows humans to choose direction for Self-realization and I-Consciousness allows them to experience bliss. Humans have a vertical spine and larger brain for awakening spiritual wisdom.

Basic human needs over history have focused on survival, pleasure, and power. The search for God or spirituality evolved over time, from belief in supernatural powers and shamanism to organized religions. This process has been typical among all nations and cultures. Each culture in history has exerted a mesmerizing influence on society. Only rare beings have been successful in transcending this influence and finding liberation. Most true spiritual leaders, artists and scientists have been visionary and ahead of their time. They have tried to share the truth instead pleasing society for personal gain. They were rejected, ignored or prosecuted during their lifetimes and were appreciated or worshipped only after they were gone.

Lord Krishna declared 4500 years ago that out of thousands perhaps one seeks liberation. This remains true today. People tend to be enmeshed in survival, pleasure, and power. Most of those who seek God or Truth are looking in the wrong direction. They are often extroverted or deluded, and remain controlled by past conditioning. Most get excited about creative ideas and practices but they cannot sustain the practice. Their enthusiasm diminishes quickly because of distractions of modern living and they lack patience. They are not true seekers.

Human life is more desirable than life in heaven. In the heavens, one enjoys all kinds of pleasures as fruits of good deeds in this world. After exhausting good merits, one has to return back to earth. Only in human life are Self-knowledge and liberation possible.

Human life is the pinnacle of evolution. A healthy body and mind are rare gifts. After many well-lived incarnations, one attains curiosity for Self-knowledge. When this curiosity ripens, one feels longing for liberation and finds the right path and the right Guru. We should not waste life just in survival and pleasure. We should utilize it for Self-Realization. Self-Realization is the most valuable attainment in human life.

Humans are more evolved and superior than animals yet they suffer from stress while animals seem to be happier. Why? Animals use their body, sense organs and mind only. These three faculties manage their life. They surrender to them and survive due to instinct. It is an effortless process. They know when and what to eat, and when to sleep. Their instinct guides them. They do not worry about tomorrow or hoard like humans. They live in the present.

Humans have the extra faculty of intellect which thinks, analyzes and chooses. Because of impure intellect and ego, one worries and plans for the future. Survival, pleasure and greed predominate. With impure intellect one chooses the wrong direction, goes against the laws of nature and suffers the consequences. The same intellect, when purified, directs one to Self-realization.

Intellect is a gift from God. All scriptures and prayers are directed toward purifying the intellect so we choose right direction in life. There are two stages of utilizing intellect.

- Primary stage: Spiritual practices start by surrendering to nature like animals to find bliss. One does not use the intellect. One allows prana to direct his or her life. Prana has built-in intelligence. It can direct body and mind efficiently if intellect does not interfere. At this stage one finds deep relaxation and freedom from stress. One learns to integrate body and mind.
- Advanced stage: At advanced levels, one purifies and sharpens intellect with meditation. This sharp intellect combined with consciousness becomes awareness. Awareness is like the sharp knife of a surgeon that can dissect a body. Awareness looks into the nature of things (Insight). This is called Vipashyana. It transforms a person. One travels inward towards the Self. Integrated body and senses with previous training helps to renounce the world. The tug of war between the world and Self ends. One reaches Atman and attains liberation and total freedom.

Liberation means removing all desires of mind, especially desires hidden as Sanskaras. Deep meditation and Samadhi burn all Sanskaras. When Sanskaras are removed, transmigration ends and one is liberated. One does not need to be born again.

## 7. PRIMARY GOAL OF LIFE

The primary goal of life is to "Know Thyself." Everyone is seeking permanent happiness called bliss. They do not know that bliss is their basic nature and seek it externally. They are running in a search outside themselves for wealth, pleasure, fame, family, love, friends and power, but ultimately find frustration instead. Everyone wants permanent happiness which can be sustained at all times and under all circumstances. This can only be achieved by searching within. Our essential nature is bliss (Anand).

Everyone is seeking immortality. Everyone wants to hold on to their possessions. People want to hold on to their health and beauty. They want their progeny to remember them like presidents who want to preserve their legacy. Yet our essential nature is eternal existence (Sat).

Everyone wants to know and control things and situations. They want to control nature and gain freedom from slavery to time and space. Yet our essential nature is consciousness (Chit) which contains all knowledge and power.

People seek happiness, immortality, and knowledge externally by using their five senses and mind. This is due to ignorance (Avidya). Due to the concealing power of Maya, they do not see Reality in front of them, and due to the projecting power of Maya, they look outside themselves. People are attracted to the world of sensations, which looks bright and attractive. They try to escape the search within by engaging in worldly activities. One can find Self by being still and realizing it directly.

We are Atman. Our basic nature is eternal existence (Sat), consciousness (Chit) and bliss (Anand). Atman is the substratum of our existence. It is like a brilliant sun that provides energy to our existence. Mind is a small reflection of it and cannot grasp it. One can comprehend Atman only being one with it. It is an individual experience and cannot be described by any language.

We can realize our true Self through stillness of mind. One has to learn to be quiet, and experience Sat Chit and Anand directly. Humans forget that everything we seek is already part of our essential nature. We do not need to do anything to find Truth, but rather become still. One has to undo instead of doing. Running and searching only takes us away from the truth. We are like the musk deer who seeks the source of fragrance, forgetting that the source is its own self. We must wake up from the dream of Maya.

Sat means eternal existence. Our existence is eternal. Atman is never born and never dies. Our body is born and dies. We change bodies as we change clothes to suit the weather. Atman has no beginning or end. It remains the same at all times and circumstances. It is the substratum of space and subtler than space. Everything appears in space yet space does not change. Fire does not burn it, water does not drench it and boundaries of buildings do not divide it. Everything other than Atman is perishable Maya. Our body looks real but did not exist 100 years ago and will be dust after 100 years. A chair looks real, but was a tree in the past and will be dust in the future. Our true existence (Atman) is Sat.

Chit means consciousness. Brahman divided itself in supreme consciousness (Purusha) and the universe (Prakriti). Supreme consciousness is all knowing intelligence, responsible for creation, sustenance and dissolution of everything in the universe. We are Atman and identical to Brahman. Everything is experienced because of consciousness. Consciousness is the subject and world is the object. Subject can exist without objects, but objects cannot exist without subject. Consciousness is like a number in front of zeros. Worldly existence is like zeros. All knowledge is reflected and revealed due to consciousness. All information may change but consciousness is a constant witness of all.

Anand means bliss. All pleasurable experiences are a mere reflection of bliss. When we deeply experience the pleasure of taste, touch, sound, smell or sight, we become introverted and experience a small measure of bliss. In ignorance we believe that it came from the external world. We try to repeat the experience by being extroverted. Happiness is a direct reflection of Atman. It comes through contact with loved ones. Exchange of Prana takes place. But this pleasure is just a diluted reflection of Atman. When we attach to things, beliefs and dogma, it gives temporary happiness or imaginary, abstract sensation of pleasure.

In reality, bliss and lasting happiness is experienced when subject, object and process becomes one. Sun is the original source of heat and light. Earth and moon merely reflect sunlight. In the same way, Self is the source of bliss, which is reflected as temporary happiness or the abstract sensation of pleasure.

Pleasure is experienced when senses connect with sense objects. It is dependent on sense objects. It diminishes in time and becomes painful after a while. Bliss is constant reservoir of peace and remains constant.

## 8. SECONDARY GOALS

One needs to support the primary goal of Self-knowledge by using secondary means. One is in human body and needs to fulfill its requirements and use them as a means to attain primary goal. We exist in the human body which is made of flesh and bones, sense organs and mind. It has to survive in the world using necessary means. Physical body is the most basic instrument for experiencing bliss.

- Physical Health: Physical health is not just a strong or shapely body but involves properly functioning brain, nervous system, cardiovascular system, digestive system, and immune system. A healthy body can prolong life and afford more years to succeed in spiritual quest.
- Mental Health: A health physical body without proper mind can be dangerous. Restless mind without proper direction can produce disasters. Mental sickness produces illusions, delusions and confusions and destroys peace. Consistent attention to inner Self produces mental health.
- Emotional Health: Emotional health plays important role in supporting primary goal. Attachment to things, people, pleasure, and one's own body produces suffering. Unconditional love expands consciousness and provides emotional health, while self-centered activities produce narrow-mindedness and loneliness.
- Money: One needs money to survive. Money purchases food, shelter and clothing for survival. Without money one becomes slave to circumstances. Moral means of earning and conserving money enable survival, pleasurable activities, and savings.
- Time: If one has health and money but no time to take a vacation, enjoy life, or find stillness and peace, one becomes a victim. Scriptures did not talk about managing time because there was no need in the past, when the pace of life was slower and business activities and social communications were less urgent.
- Wisdom: One needs wisdom to balance health, money and time. Without proper wisdom a healthy and wealthy person with available time may misuse resources, become a drug addict, or commit suicide.

## 9. THE IMPORTANCE OF WISDOM

For a successful journey we need a goal, proper direction, and proper means for travel. Goal remains the same. We need to change means as necessary. One may use a car, boat or plane as suitable for the journey. But do not hang on to the means. When you cross the river, let go of the boat. Once the goal is set do not worry when you will reach there. Just enjoy the journey. Take necessary detours, short cuts or rest. Keep your eyes on the road to see the proper distance ahead.

Our primary goal is to attain bliss. Everything is only means. We should consider means as a secondary goal and set tertiary means to attain it. For example; money is a secondary goal. Being efficient and sacrificing comforts and pleasure to earn money is called tertiary means. Many people get lost in the means and forget the primary goal.

A formula can be used to understand this concept. If attaining Self-knowledge requires 100 points, physical health would contribute 10 points, mental health 10 points, emotional health 10 points, money 15 points, time 15 points, and wisdom 40 points.

his shows clearly that those who spend lots of energy and time earning money gain relatively few benefits. In the process of making money, they become workaholics, slaves to working. They sacrifice their health and family life in attaining financial success. They get conditioned and lose capacity to be still and enjoy life.

One should work to generate a surplus of money. This will reduce stress and allow more time for Self-Realization. One also has to manage time efficiently. One can cut down on unnecessary activities to gain surplus of time. One should also preserve energy so it is available for spiritual practices.

One can acquire more benefits by gaining wisdom than by acquiring any other resource. For example, wisdom supports positive actions that help preserve physical, emotional and mental health. Wisdom can help one survive more easily and efficiently. The formula also gives us direction that we should spend more time gaining wisdom than working merely to survive. Also, one may possess the basic necessities needed to survive, such as food and clean water, but lack the wisdom needed to use them properly.

Health, money and time can replace each other, but nothing can replace wisdom. Wisdom is needed to balance all aspects of life. What does one need to gain wisdom? How much time does one need to attain wisdom? It takes only awareness. One does not need to sacrifice anything. One can gain this awareness at any age and any physical condition.

Wisdom is attained when be become still and quiet, and realize we are free. It is the process of waking up from Maya. One needs constant Satsang to keep awareness alive.

## ✓ 10. WISDOM AND SPIRITUAL DISCERNMENT (VIVEK)

Vivek means to be able to distinguish permanent from impermanent and real from unreal. One has to purify intellect to attain Vivek. Intellect is purified by removing restlessness of mind through meditation and spiritual austerities. Mind becomes pure and sharp like surgeon's knife to cut through darkness of ignorance and attachments.

Purified mind develops intuition. Intuition is not limited by logic but gives vision beyond the boundaries of time and space. Intuition gives us guidance in life. With intuition, one sees reality as unified existence instead of names and forms. One sees all objects, living creatures and own body as nothing but vibrations of five subtle basic elements (Earth, water, fire, air and space).

Vivek is the essence of Vipashyana (Vipassana in Pali language) meditation. Sometimes it is called insight meditation or mindfulness. With direct perception, one loses attachments to things and people and sees the oneness of all. One sees all being as varieties of changing waves, yet part of the same ocean. This is true renunciation (Vairagya). One does not struggle to renounce. Rather, with deep insight, attachments fall away naturally.

With wisdom and discernment, the following steps will ensure proper direction in life:

- Set Priorities: One needs clarity in order to set priorities. One wastes time and energy without setting priorities. Priorities allow you to move more quickly in the right direction.
- Be Visionary: One should avoid being short-sighted or impulsive. Being visionary gives one a panoramic view of life. It is like seeing the view from a helicopter when stuck in the traffic jam. Most people suffer because they are impulsive. They are programmed due to conditioning and cannot think outside the box.
- Flow with Life: One needs to be flexible and adjust to changing situations of life. One can get stuck or attached

to things and suffer the consequences. Being able to flow with life feeds spiritual undercurrent.

- Recognize the Permanence of Self: One has to understand that Self is the subject and world is the object. World revolves around Self. Subject can exist without objects but objects can exist only due to Self. Self is like a number in front of zeros. Self is permanent reality while world changes constantly.

- Realize Self is the Source of Happiness: Self alone can give permanent happiness while world can give only temporary pleasure followed by pain. Even heaven can be experienced only because of Self.

- Practice Unconditional Love: Communicate with everyone with love instead of being caught up in petty attachments. Consider life as a privilege.

- Be Self-Reliant: Rely on Self and intuition instead of public opinion and sensory input. Do not follow blindly. To hang on to someone else is only a temporary escape.

- Understand the Law of Karma: The entire universe is connected. Cause and effect, and duty (Dharma) regulates entire universe with perfect order and justice: "What you sow, so shall you reap."

- Please the Self: Try to please your higher Self instead of pampering your senses or pleasing others.

- Recognize the Nature of Mind: Realize that mind can be the cause of bondage or freedom.

- Be Alone with Self: We are alone with our self from birth to death. No one can eat for us, dream for us, take away our pain or die for us. Others can only inspire or guide us. We cannot do anything for anyone but serve unconditionally with love and compassion. Take responsibility for your actions.

- Witness Life (Drishta): Recognize that we are not the doer (Karta) or enjoyer (Bhokta) but only a witness (Sakshi). God creates, sustains and dissolves the universe.

## 11. REALITY OF NOW

Reality is here and now. One needs to be in the present to enjoy life or transform life. If one is driving at a high speed, one cannot enjoy the scenery. If one is pre-occupied with worries, one cannot enjoy a meal at a fancy restaurant. If one is pre-occupied with survival, pleasure or power one cannot focus inward and get to know Self. Reality is experienced only by being in the present. Hindrances to the experience of reality are conditioning of the past, illusions of the future and trying to escape through restless activities in the present.

How can we be in the present? Mind is restless like a monkey that is drunk and has been bitten by a scorpion. Yet it can be tamed like wild animals are trained. We can remain in the present with deep relaxation and awareness.

For practical purposes, one can remain in the present, witness all situations in life and recognize world as a cosmic dream. The ultimate goal of life is to attain Self-Realization and reach eternal Reality.

Permanent reality is perceived in deepest meditation called Samadhi. Samadhi is total absorption of mind. One should withdraw attention from the external world and focus on Atman deep within spiritual heart. Atman is the ultimate Reality and source of energy and consciousness. When electricity goes out it returns to the power house. When we withdraw senses and mind it returns to Atman. Atman is eternal consciousness without boundaries or duality of time and space. Scriptures explain this eternal consciousness and techniques to attain it.

According to Vedanta Philosophy we exist in three states of consciousness that contradict each other: Waking (Jagrat), dream (Swapna) and deep sleep (Susupti). One needs to transcend these and attain the fourth state (Turiya) in deep Samadhi.

- Waking state (Jagrat): During waking state, consciousness uses body, senses and mind to experience the world in the present. It is more predominant and longer than dream reality. But in relation to ultimate awakening, it is merely a longer dream.
- Dream state (Swapna): During dream state, consciousness uses senses and mind without the presence of the body. One can travel in the past and future and work out

conflicts of the waking state.

- Deep sleep (Susupti): During deep sleep, consciousness is disconnected from body, senses and mind. One loses awareness of pleasure, pain and time. One remembers nothing but feels revived after deep sleep. Dream state and deep sleep alternate at about two hour intervals. Dreams release tension and deep sleep refreshes us. Both are mechanisms of nature needed for our survival. If dream state or deep sleep is interrupted, our state of health will be disturbed.

- Transcendental state (Turiya): Turiya means the fourth state of consciousness. It is also called Samadhi. It is the state of eternal consciousness without beginning and end. Waking and dreaming states are temporary states of consciousness while deep sleeping state is the temporary blockage of consciousness. All three states give conflicting experiences, while the transcendental state remains a witness of them all and remains untouched by them. Turiya is the substratum of all states of consciousness and covers them all. It finds no conflict with other states of consciousness. It is the source of Peace.

Deep sleep and Samadhi both look similar on the surface because consciousness is withdrawn from body, senses and the mind. However, consciousness is covered with ignorance in deep sleep and the experience does not change a person. In Samadhi, one gets connected with Supreme Consciousness and wakes up with wisdom that transforms his or her life.

According to Yogi Patanjali, mind exists as thought waves (Chitta) that fluctuates due to five kinds of thought wave pattern (Chitta vrittis). When one restrains them, original nature is experienced. Original nature is Self (Atman) and experiences bliss. These five thought waves are:

- Direct perception (Praman) or experience through sensory input. One sees an actual snake on the path or a real lake in the distance (Pratyaksha). One also gets real information by inference (Anuman). One sees smoke and knows there is fire without actually seeing the fire.

- Illusion (Viparyaya): One perceives wrong information due to illusion. One sees snake in a rope or water in a mirage.
- Delusion (Vikalpa): One believes something that does not exist. For instance, one perceives images without substance. One gets images due to spoken words.
- Deep sleep (Nidra): One experiences peace in deep sleep but cannot remember the experience. One only remembers having a good sleep.
- Memory (Smriti): One remembers past experiences during dreams and recalling the past when day dreaming.

Our thought waves change during waking, dreaming and slumber states of consciousness. In the waking state, mind perceives reality directly or by inference. Sometimes it perceives wrong information (Illusion) and sometimes it imagines what does not exist (Delusion). In dreams and day dreams it perceives different realities. In deep sleep, consciousness gets covered up with ignorance and feels bliss of ignorance. Bliss of ignorance is like a car with head lights at the top of a hill. The light is present yet does not reflect without a road ahead. Bliss of ignorance is like a drunken person who temporarily forgets his problems. Yet the problems do not go away. When one transcends all five modifications of mind (Chitta), one attains stillness and finds lasting bliss.

Reality is eternal existence. Vedanta calls it Samadhi when one transcends three lower states of consciousness. Yogi Patanjali describes it as removing the five kinds of mental waves (Chitta vritti) to become established in Self. Lord Krishna describes the removal of all cravings of mind and becoming content in the Self. Lord Buddha says desires are the root cause of bondage. The hindrances to liberation are conditioning of the past, illusion of the future and escapes in the present.

## 12. CONDITIONING OF THE PAST

We are born with innocence and purity. We are conditioned by our parents and are indoctrinated into various religions during childhood. We are programmed to accept certain value systems, and concepts about happiness, morality, diet and lifestyle. We are programmed by schools, priests, politicians and news media. We are programmed and accept without questioning concepts of God, good and evil, moral and immoral, heaven and hell.

These days we are bombarded with news media, politicians and changing trends. Constant bombardment hypnotizes us and we believe what we are told without thinking. News media distorts our perception and we lose the capacity to think and choose. Politicians are the representation of collective consciousness of society. If the society is not spiritually evolved, it will choose a politician based upon their short sighted impulses and rely on his promises instead of looking at his personal character. People believe in unattainable promises of politicians because they are constantly bombarded and brain washed by the speech of politicians which satisfies their fantasy. Politicians often contradict their promises after being elected. People get adjusted to the lies.

Spiritual leaders and spiritual movements are also results of collective consciousness of people. Masses of people want escapes, miracles and quick fix. This encourages con artists to become spiritual leaders. Anyone who has talent and desire to be popular invent new ways to attract crowds with their speech. Some of them perform magic tricks and people are fooled that they performed miracles. People are attached to their path and feel threatened by knowing the truth.

Vedic teachings are more than 5000 years old. Teachings were corrupted by rituals and animal sacrifices by priests for their gain. Lord Buddha and Mahavira 2500 years ago revolted and established new direction with love, non-violence, and compassion. It turned into religion and became corrupt again. Aadi Shankaracharya revived Vedic teachings again in year 800 AD. His teachings became corrupt and produced escapist misusing the concept of Maya. Guru Nanak revived the concept of Dharma in 1500 AD by being strong and defending the country. It produced Sikh religion. It became corrupt. They started fight against Hinduism.

All ancient teachings become corrupt and become religion. Judaism which is 5000 year old is the foundation of Christianity

2000 years ago and Islam 1400 years ago. Yet they consider themselves separate and establish cults within the religion. Vedic culture is the foundation of Hinduism, Buddhism, Jainism and Sikhism. Yet they isolate themselves as unique religion.

Experiences in life program us to experience positive feelings, negative feelings and combinations of both. We become prejudiced about our own nation, religion, culture and race. People born in communist countries are mesmerized by the culture and take dictatorship for granted. They cannot think about freedom of speech. People born in the families with dogma or fanaticism inherit those beliefs. We are programmed to be perfect. Competition is encouraged. This produces stress. We are programmed to try to look good to others instead of feeling good within. We are born with subconscious impressions and hidden memories of past lives (Sanskaras). We retain deep desires, intention, and free will in the current life. The accumulated Sanskaras of previous lives become our personality (Swabhav). We are influenced by various social environments. Their influences mold our lives. Constant bombardment of stimulus hypnotizes us and traps us.

During our recent trip to India, we noticed that people are conditioned and stuck. Men are programmed to sit and give orders to wife and children. Helping out or getting their own glass of water is considered below their dignity. Many poor families hire a maid to sweep the floor, and do laundry and dishes. This is expensive and people become dependent on the maid. I tried to help with chores and tried to show them that no one is above daily chores such as cutting the lawn or vacuuming the floor.

Many women in India are involved in ritualistic worship, chanting religious texts without knowing the meaning. They have temple in the house to worship their idol by feeding, clothing and putting deity to sleep. When they go away, they assign their ritualistic worship to a neighbor. They run to their temple several times a day. Their idea of purity is taking bath instead internal purity. This is taken for granted. They do not find concentration or peace of mind. It provides only social activities and escapes.

They follow religious fasts to achieve some spiritual merits in the future or in heaven. Instead of water fast, they can do fruit fast. They follow traditional fast instead. They substitute normal foods with mostly starchy and unhealthy foods. They break the fast on Krishna's birthday at midnight with a feast after a whole day's fast. This diminishes the physical benefits of fasting.

On the positive side, people in India are deeply influenced by their spiritual heritage, by morality and the law of Karma. They tend to share unconditionally and maintain family ties. Even poor families maintain joint family system and learn sharing and sacrificing. Talking and sharing personal issues with neighbors and even with a stranger is commonly accepted practice. One removes tensions by sharing and avoids the need for psychotherapy.

Most children grow up in a secure environment despite poverty, with love from siblings, uncles and aunties. This childhood security gives stability and contentment in adult life. Crimes and shootings are rare. There is a subtle sense of security in the air. Students still respect teachers. Necessity has created many virtues. People have learned to be patient in traffic jams and long lines. Small crimes and accidents are resolved spontaneously instead of through the courts. People have learned to use small places effectively for business and residence. Resources are used effectively, items are repaired rather than repurchased, and there is hardly any need to recycle. People have learned to be content, but this is changing rapidly with Western influences.

Such changes are happening all over the world. Traditional societies are changing as new technologies and ideologies take hold. In the U.S., people take prosperity, independence and comforts for granted. Children have their own rooms, televisions and phones. Personal privacy and selfishness have created isolation. Neighbors remain strangers. In many families, people maintain privacy and do not talk or communicate. It builds tensions and creates need for psychotherapy. People are busy with computers and smart phones and have lost capacity to communicate directly. Dependence on gadgets instead of thinking has diminished capacity to think creatively. Family unity is disappearing. People have become intolerant and have lost patience. There are broken marriages due to intolerance, selfishness instead of sacrifice, lack of communication and possessive attachments. There are frequent road rages and shootings. Democracy works properly when society maintains moral and spiritual values. Strong boundaries between people have encouraged lawsuits for petty crimes. Teachers are afraid of students.

There are distractions and discontentment in spite of abundance. Combination of abundance and freedom without understanding is destroying family structure and compassion. Many young people from broken homes around the world become insecure, listen to terrorist propaganda and become home grown terrorists. People experience fear and insecurity due to unexpected threats. With constant media bombardment of threats of various kinds, people are programmed (Sanskaras) to fear, causing stress, restlessness and other psychosomatic problems. One can break away from conditioning only by thinking, questioning and taking responsibility for one's own life.

## 13. ILLUSIONS OF THE FUTURE

We are under the spell of cosmic illusion (Maya) and we do not know it. A dream is real as long as we are dreaming. When we wake up from the spell of Maya, world will disappear. All the names and forms are illusion. The world we experience is relatively real, but in absolute terms it is unreal. Maya means what we perceive with senses and mind is unreal, but the consciousness (Atman) which is invisible is real.

Illusions distort reality. We often see and believe what pleases us. It takes us away from reality and experience of the present.

Some illusions of Maya: We see a snake in a coiled rope. We see waves, bubbles, foam and ocean instead of water. We see ornaments instead of gold. We see a movie on the screen instead of the screen. We see beads on a necklace instead of the string that supports them. We see mirages in the desert.

- Illusion of tomorrow: We look forward to being happy when external situations change. Reality is in the present. If we cannot be happy today, we cannot be happy tomorrow.
- Illusion that happiness comes from outside: Happiness is our basic nature. Searching only disturbs it. Grass always looks greener from a distance.
- Illusion of being lucky: Law of karma determines

outcome. We gain what we deserve. Life will be wasted in waiting. Even if you become lucky, it will only bring miseries.

- Illusion of being immortal: We forget that body ages and will die, yet people hoard as if they are immortal.
- Illusion of pleasure: Pleasure comes from sense stimulation when we become introverted. It gives illusion as if it came from senses. All pleasures drain energy.
- Illusion of wisdom: We think that reading books and listening to discourses will bring wisdom. Wisdom comes from meditation, introspection and living with awareness.
- Illusion of love: We get attached in name of love (Moha). In reality, attachments exist in the mind and shrink our consciousness, while love is the experience of heart and expands consciousness.
- Illusion of cures: We think food, exercises and medicines cure diseases. In reality they allow energy to flow and Prana does the healing.
- Illusion of enlightenment: One practices severe austerities to find enlightenment. One blindly follows Gurus and offers prayers to God for enlightenment. In reality, we have to realize that we are already enlightened. We have to be still and realize it.

While in India in 2017, we noticed people taking vows to sacrifice comforts so they might be rewarded in this life or in heaven. They offer cocoanut, fruits and flowers to deity and ask for precious gifts, thinking they can bargain with God.

Many villagers dislike animals. Cows and dogs roam wildly in the streets. Cows eat plastic due to starvation and die. However, on special assigned holy day once a year, they worship dogs and cows and overfeed them. The animals get sick or die from overeating. People worship cows as holy mother, but leave them loose on the street when they stop giving milk. They pay priests to pray for their ancestors to watch over them and to grant good luck. Priests invent techniques to extort money from desperate clients. Rich people give charitable donations to the temples but ignore their workers and neighbors. Temple donation is usually misused.

Illusion is present in all religions and cultures. It is human nature to look in the future for happiness. Most religions talk about heaven and hell. Temptation of heaven and fear of hell are used to promote their religion. There is no geographical location of heaven or hell, yet people are occupied with future instead of improving their present. Popular illusion in the U.S. is participating in lottery for a jackpot. Only a few survive the shock of winning a jackpot. Most people get trapped in problems. Most Americans are influenced by commercials and have become impulsive buyers and cannot catch up with debts. Entire economy is based on impulsive nature of people. Many people do not maintain savings for retirement.

## 14. ESCAPES IN THE PRESENT

After you remove conditioning of the past and illusions of the future, you have to utilize present to explore Self. You can enjoy beauty only when you are still and in the present.

One has to practice aloneness of Self. Connecting with Self gives inner strength to withstand the distractions of the world. One becomes lonely when disconnected from the Self. Activities cannot fill the gap.

One runs outward because of impurities of mind (Mala). Impurities cover the clarity just like dirt covers a mirror and algae covers a lake. Impurities obstruct vision.

One runs away from the Self due to veiling power of Maya (Aavaran). Veiling power hides Self and one gets lost in the darkness of Maya. This darkness is spiritual blindness (Avidya). One sees impermanent as permanent, pain as pleasure, impure as pure and non-self as Self.

One also runs away from Self due to projecting power of Maya (Vikshep). One sees attraction in external world and uses Ego (Asmita) to experience it. One is attracted to pleasure (Raga) and has aversion (Dwesha) to pain. This vacillation and running from one to the other produces frustration.

There is deep-rooted fear of death (Abhinivesh) in all living creatures. This fear manifests in strange ways. Fear of death reflects into secondary fears and insecurities such as loss of money, shelter, job, or loved ones. One creates imaginary fears and runs outside to cover up the fear.

People are afraid to be alone with the Self. They find darkness within and brightness in the world outside. They invent activities, parties, gossips, shopping, smart phones and computers to occupy themselves. Some take shelter in drugs or alcohol. Some run after money, fame or power. People run in circles unconsciously and get frustrated. Some run as Gurus or leaders and some run as disciples or followers. Some run outside to attain material success and some run outside to attain spiritual success.

Materialistic people are asleep to spiritual activities while spiritual people remain asleep to material pursuits. Many people participate in spiritual activities to fulfill material ambitions and to build ego. They are hypocrites. One needs to be quiet and content to experience the bliss of Self. Material pursuits can be directed to achieve this primary goal.

We noticed that many people in contemporary India are malnourished due to poverty. This is understandable. But wealthy people have the choice to be healthy. Yet, so many of them are out of shape. They are at risk from many diseases of the West. They escape the need to maintain personal health and the search for Truth by going to fancy restaurants and indulging in wealthy luxuries. They experience temporary enjoyment by showing off their wealth, building fancy houses, throwing parties and giving to charities for recognition and power.

People in all nations and all cultures find ways to escape the present. Churches, temples and synagogues provide mostly social life and have become commercial institutions. Followers focus on the means rather than the goal of Self knowledge. People do as they are told and do not question authorities. They follow severe austerities prescribed by their religions to torture their bodies and mind as an escape or to inflate ego instead of knowing the scientific reason for personal disciplines. All religions have broken into sects and dogmas. Hinduism has more sects than other religious with many Gods, demi-Gods and Goddesses. Each sect has its own temples, moral rules, festivities and life style.

Sects of same religion compete with each other. Most wars are fought in the name of religion. People revolve around the external religion rather than their own experience of Self. Such escapes cover up inner insecurities and affirm ego. As one evolves, one finds unity, experiences contentment, and feels no need to escape.

# PART 2: MEDITATION PRACTICE

## 1. THE CHART: DIRECTION IN LIFE

The entire universe is nothing but unified field of consciousness. It is the substratum of existence. It is called Brahman. It is eternal. It is without beginning and without boundaries. It reflects as Atman (Soul) in all living creatures big and small and everything visible or invisible. Brahman and Atman are qualitatively the same. Everyone and everything within Brahman are only reflections of the Source and change constantly. This reflection is called Maya or cosmic illusion.

Brahman is the dancer and entire universe is dance. Dancer is part of the dance. This is divine play of God (Leela). This means everything and everyone is permeated with God consciousness.

We are all co-creators of our destiny. We are covered up with layers of causal body, astral body and gross body. Causal body is I-consciousness and is all pervading. Astral body is made of mind and intellect while gross body is made of matter and sense organs (Energy). God's energy reflects first to consciousness, then to mind and body.

Everyone appears separated from God by Maya. The journey back to the Source is called evolution. Meditation is an introverted journey. It gives peace and freedom in proportion to introversion. Meditation and spiritual practices quicken evolution until we realize our essential nature. However, masses of people are extroverted. They use their sense organs to experience the world and seek happiness. They produce attachment to persons and things, and extend further outward, identifying with various dogmas, religions, culture and nations.

We use our internal organs of mind (Manah), intellect (Buddhi), I-Consciousness (Ahankar) and unconscious mind (Chitta) to direct our life. These four faculties working together are called Antahkaran. We use our body and sense organs to experience the world. In the process of experiencing the world, we get lost and forget our divine nature. This is called bondage. If we live with awareness and realize our essential nature as pure consciousness, we become free. This is called liberation (Moksha).

Body is like a chariot, the five senses are like five horses. Mind is the reins and intellect is the chauffer. Self is the master riding the chariot. Life is the journey. Self-Realization is the destination. Master has to be awake to order the chauffer. Intellect has to control five senses and direct them properly using the mind. Mind and senses have to be strong and alert. Body has to be strong. Decorating the body instead of maintaining it will cause problems.

Atman is covered up with five layers of ignorance (Sheaths). Ignorance has no connection with education or college degree. Ignorance means lack of awareness of Self (Atman). Outer to inner layers covering (Sheaths) of Atman are: body, senses, mind, intellect, I-Consciousness and unconscious mind (Chitta).

I-Consciousness is called Causal body and is most pervasive of all. Intellect and mind are called Astral body. Senses and body parts are called Gross body. Gross body is limited by time and space.

These three bodies function together. Gross body is like an ice cube, astral body is like water and causal body is like vapor. Gross body is used during waking hours, astral body is used during thinking and dreaming and causal body is used during contemplation.

## UNDERSTANDING THE CHART

- Body (Sharir): Body is made of flesh, bones and blood. It is sustained by food and return to earth at the end. It is called Annamaya kosha which the grossest of all
- Energy (Prana): Prana pervades entire universe and entire body. Its energy allows five sense organs and five motor

organs to function. It is called Pranamaya Kosha.

- Mind (Manah): Mind is nothing but bundle of thoughts. Mind is born when we pay attention to thoughts. Its function is to register experiences received by the senses like a camera. It is called Manomaya Kosha. Intense feelings in the mind are called emotions.

- Intellect (Buddhi): Buddhi is the discriminating faculty of the mind. It judges and analyzes. It is subtler than the mind. It is called Vignanamaya Kosha.

- I-Consciousness (Ahankar): Ahankar means pure ego or I-consciousness. It remains in the background as a witness. It is subtler than intellect. It is called Anandmaya Kosha. It does not think or analyze. When it is identified with body or mind, it becomes contaminated and is called Ego.

- Unconscious Mind (Chitta): It is unconscious mind. It stores impressions. These impressions are called Sanskaras. Sanskaras survive death. Sanskaras control our life. Chitta is like hidden part of an iceberg. It is not shown in the Chart.

- Internal Faculties (Antahkaran): Combination of mind, intellect, I- Consciousness and unconscious mind is called Antahkaran, which directs our life.

- Supreme Self (Parmatma): Atman/ Brahman are called Supreme Self. It is the substratum of entire universe. It provides energy to causal, astral and gross bodies. Human mind cannot comprehend Supreme Self. It is like a shinning sun. It is self-sustained reservoir. One does not need a flash of light to see the sun.

- Soul (Jivatma): I-Consciousness using body, senses, mind and intellect is called Jivatma. (I and ME in the chart is called Jivatma.)

- World (Jagat): People, living creatures and things are called Jagat (Mine and Ours in the chart are called Jagat).

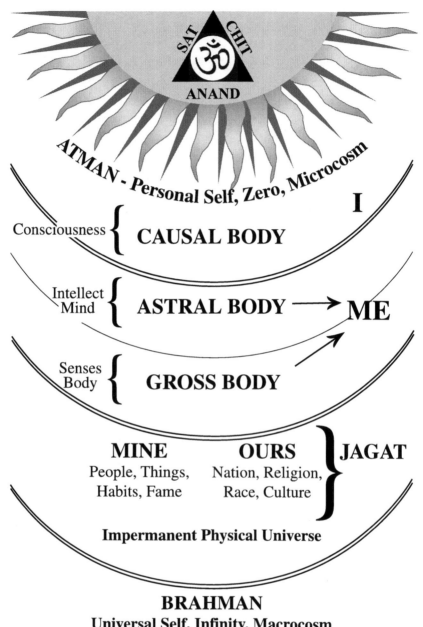

ATMAN - Personal Self, Zero, Microcosm

I

Consciousness { **CAUSAL BODY**

Intellect
Mind { **ASTRAL BODY** ⟶ **ME**

Senses
Body { **GROSS BODY**

**MINE**          **OURS**      } **JAGAT**
People, Things,   Nation, Religion,
Habits, Fame      Race, Culture

**Impermanent Physical Universe**

**BRAHMAN**
**Universal Self, Infinity, Macrocosm**

**AUM Vibration**

Jivatma has two choices: World or Supreme Self. If it gets tangled in the world it gets in bondage. If it goes inward towards Parmatma, it finds liberation. Jivatma can experience the world with awareness and recognize it as Maya. Then it wakes up from Maya to find liberation.

Atman/Brahman. Atman and Brahman are identical. Looking from personal view, Brahman looks like Atman. Atman is eternal. It has no beginning or boundaries. It is never born and never dies. It is the substratum of the universe. It covers everyone and everything. It is self-effulgent like the sun and gives life to causal, astral and gross bodies. One does not need flash light to see the sun. Mind is part of it but has no capacity to perceive it. It can be experienced only when one transcends the mind. This experience is personal and cannot be described by words. Vedas describe it by saying "Not this, not this (Neti, neti)" Direct experiences of spiritual masters are described in Upanishads. Upanishads only give us guidelines. One has to follow the teachings to experience it personally.

- I in the chart refers to I-Consciousness
- ME in the chart refers to combination on body, senses, mind and intellect.
- MINE in chart refers to our possessions of material things, relatives and fame.
- OURS in chart refers to our abstract belonging to nation, religion, race and culture.

Functions of our faculties: Body is the field in which all faculties function. Five sense organs perceive information. Mind registers it. Mind uses brain to allow five motor organs to function. When one experiences sensation of pleasure or pain, intellect is born. Intellect judges and analyzes situations. With judgment, the feeling of I AM is born. When I AM produces feeling of separation, dichotomy of subject and objects are born. I becomes the subject and world becomes the object. One identifies own self with body, senses and mind and becomes Jivatma. Jivatma tries to preserve personal identity. It perceives pleasure and pain. When Jivatma interprets experiences as pleasant or unpleasant, it registers impressions (Sanskaras) in unconscious mind (Chitta). Intensity and attachments determine the depth of Sanskaras. We constantly produce Sanskaras through our experiences of the world. These Sanskaras control our life. These Sanskaras survive death. One uses the world to fulfill desires. It causes transmigration. Transmigration is considered bondage. When one removes all Sanskaras in deep Samadhi, one is liberated from transmigration.

Mechanism of experiences in life: When someone throws a ball at you, eyes see and ears hear, mind recognizes that as an object. Intellect analyzes the object and determines that it is a round ball. I-consciousness identifies itself as body and becomes subject and ball becomes the object. One tries to protect the body from being injured. One gets injured anyway. Ball coming at you is the cause Injury is the effect. The painful experience registers in the unconscious mind as Sanskar. Person may be more aware next time and moves more quickly to avoid injury. This is evolution.

### The Chart Explains All Basic Teachings of Scriptures
- Vedanta Philosophy of Upanishads: Vedanta philosophy teaches that Brahman is ultimate reality. Maya covers it with cosmic illusion. The goal is to rise above Maya by using Maya to realize Brahman. In the chart, causal body, astral body and gross bodies are the coverings of Maya. One removes Maya with the following tools. Vivek (Spiritual discernment). Vairagya (Renunciation). Mumuksha (Desire for liberation). Shat sampatti (Six virtues): Tranquility of mind, control of senses, mental poise, forbearance, faith and surrender.
- Sankhya Yoga of Kapila: Sankhya philosophy describes that Brahman projects himself as consciousness (Purusha) and his energy Prakriti). Purusha and prakriti unite together to create universe made of 24 elements. In the chart, everything other than Brahman is made of 24 elements. One transcends these elements to realize Brahman.
- Raja Yoga (Royal path) of Yogi Patanjali: Raja Yoga has eight limbs. Its goal is union with Brahman. One uses Ten

Commandments of Yamas and Niyamas to be in rhythm with Jagat. One uses Yoga positions and breathing to gain mastery of gross body. One uses sense withdrawal, concentration and meditation to gain mastery over astral body and practices Samadhi to gain mastery over causal body. In Samadhi, one attains union with Brahman.

- Meditation: Meditation is the inward journey from Jagat to Brahman using any path as a means. One removes the attachments of the world. Then remove attachments to gross and astral bodies and reaches I-Consciousness and Atman/Brahman.

## 2. MEDITATION AND AFFIRMATIONS

Do not be confused with commercial contamination of the word meditation. Meditation is simple, easy and accessible to all at any age, physical condition or time of day. One can sit quietly for passive meditation or apply it during daily activities.

In the chart in the previous section, you can see that Atman is covered with layers of intellect, mind, senses and body. It extends further to MINE and OURS. Reversing the journey back to the Source is meditation.

Raja yoga is the most scientific approach to meditation. It offers eight-fold path to Liberation. Ideally one should change lifestyle and practice morality, strengthen the body with yoga positions and breathing, then practice sense withdrawal, concentration and meditation. These are steps and tools. However, you can also practice basic meditation for immediate benefits.

Mind is connected with breath. When breath slows down, mind also slows down. Meditation is not for making mind blank but slowing down mind's activities. Active mind functions at beta wave frequency. When it becomes quiet, it functions at alpha wave frequency. You may not recognize when you are in a meditative state. When mind is quiet, it becomes introverted and gets in touch with consciousness and Atman. It finds peace, relaxation, inspiration and guidance. With constant and rhythmic practice, you notice benefits. After sleep you wake up without any changes. After meditation, you wake up with deeper wisdom. At times, quantum leap can occur. Mind is receptive while in meditative state. Our unconscious mind (Chitta) stores impressions of this lifetime and previous incarnations. These Sanskaras control our life. During deep relaxation you can use affirmations to reprogram unconscious mind. Harsh disciplines and intellectual information does not control our life but Sanskaras control them. Harsh disciplines cannot be sustained for a long time because old conditioning surfaces and controls us. Affirmations tame mind and old habits like taming wild animals. Affirmations are phrases with deep positive meaning which are recited or thought about to make deep impression on the mind. They can be recited aloud, then whispered and ultimately recited silently in the mind. This influences gross, astral and causal bodies. When influence reaches Chitta, it makes dynamic changes in life effortlessly.

## 3. SIMPLE PASSIVE MEDITATION PRACTICE

Sit in any comfortable position in quiet environment free from distractions. Remove previous ideas about meditation. Observe the breath passively. Do not try to do breathing or control breathing. Observe the breath and travel with it. Mentally travel in when breath flows in and travel out with outgoing breath. Your consciousness will become part of breathing process. You will feel the journey of the breath. You will notice breathing becoming slower and rhythmic. Generally, breathing involves 15 or more breaths per minute. It will slow down to 10 breaths or less per minute. You do not need to worry about it. It gives you confidence by knowing it. Because of old habit, mind will forget paying attention and will start thinking again. This is normal. Do not fight. As soon as you realize it, get back to observing the breath. Mind will slow down and will give some visible benefits after regular practice. Practice twice a day for fifteen minutes. This is only the guideline. There are no hard rules. Results are attained by steady persistent practice.

Mind gets used to being quiet. You will experience subtle joy different than familiar pleasure of the senses. This experience will inspire you to continue your practice. This experience is due to stillness of mind and connection with consciousness and Atman. The experiences should not be the driving force but rather commitment to sit regularly without looking for any rewards. There is nothing tangible to attain by meditation but to drop imaginary burdens of the mind. At times experiences of meditation are unpleasant because Sanskaras are released. Do not be attached to the experiences. Just observe them and witness them.

Variation 1: Pay attention to the beginning and end part of the breath after you have succeeded in the practice. It slows down and makes transition. Mind slows down proportionately. When the breath stops during transition, you transcend the mind and experience bliss.

Variation 2: Travel with the breath and visualize travelling in and out with the breath. When you travel in, go to the innermost chamber of your heart until you become zero. This is the experience of Atman. When you travel out, go out in the space, expanding until your mind dissolves. This is the experience of Brahman. Atman and Brahman are identical.

Travelling in, you become zero and travelling out you become infinity. Both times you transcend the mind. Zero is infinity because there is no time or space to compare. This is meditation where subject, object and process become one. Traveling with breath provides concentration while both ends provide meditation. Stay for several minutes to register the experience in the Chitta. You can recall the peaceful experience anytime during the day. Whenever you recall the experience, it deepens.

At the end of meditation recite some of the following affirmations. You can say aloud or in your mind. After each affirmation, reflect on its deep essence and get to the depth of it.

## 4. ATTUNEMENT, NEGATIONS, AFFIRMATIONS AND EXPANSIONS

After meditation you may recite personal attunements, negations, affirmations and expansions. Personal attunement opens one up for personal transformation. Negations remove or eliminate all illusions. Affirmations confirm reality and help one to experience bliss. Expansions spread the bliss experience.

### Personal Attunement
- I accept myself.
- I love myself.
- I love life and the creation of God.

- I forgive all beings and pray for their well-being.
- I thank God for all the gifts of life.
- I accept these gifts as privileges.
- I am created in the image of God.
- The Lord is my guide and companion.
- Health and happiness are my birth rights.
- I deserve the grace of God.
- I take responsibility for all the situations in my life.
- I accept all the challenges of life with a smiling face.
- I am willing to grow and transform myself.
- The entire world is my family.
- I am willing to share my bliss with the world.

"Who am I?" is the basic question. Meditate on it. It takes questioning and rejecting that which you are not. What remains is the reality of Self

### Negations to Eliminate Illusion
Breathe in normally. Breathe out through the mouth effortlessly with a gentle sound of relief. Empty out the following negations and feel relief and weightlessness.

### Ours:
- I have no race or nationality. The human race is my nationality.
- I have no religion. Dharma is my universal religion.
- I have no dogma or belief. Divine light removes my ignorance.

### Mine:
- I have no family. All living creatures are my family members.
- I have no home. The entire universe is my home.
- I have no fame or power. All I have is a small reflection of the divine.
- I own nothing. All my needs are provided by the divine.
- I possess no one. I am here to serve others for my

purification and evolution.

- I control nothing. I am an instrument. Cosmic law governs everything.
- I rely on nothing and no one. I rely on divine grace and satsang.

**Me:**

- I have no name. Name is just a label.
- I am not a father, brother, son, mother or sister. These are the roles I play.
- I am not male or female. I am the spirit without boundaries.
- I am not the body. It is vibrating energy that changes constantly.
- I am not the senses. They are only the means of perception and action.
- I am not the mind. The mind does not exist. The mind is changing waves.
- I am free from duality. Free from pleasure-pain, gain-loss, honor-insult.
- I am not emotions. They change constantly.
- I am not intellect. I rely on divine guidance and intuition.

### Affirmations to Confirm Bliss

Before you practice the following affirmations, focus on Atman located within spiritual heart. Spiritual heart is located where you feel your true being, in the middle of chest.

**I:**

- I am the Self (Atman), the spark of God as sat, chit and anand.
- I am bliss consciousness, an uninvolved passive witness to the drama of life.
- I am immortal, never born, never dying. I am sustained by the divine energy.
- I have nothing to attain, nothing to be, nowhere to go.
- I am perfect, self sufficient, content. I need nothing added

to life.

- I am perfect and free here and now. Nothing or no one binds me.

## Expansions To Spread Bliss Experience

Not all children have the same age, talent, aptitude or physical condition. But they are perfect in themselves and evolve at their own level. Humans have evolved to the highest level of consciousness.

All creation has different names and forms but their basic constitution is made of the same five basic elements: earth, water, fire, air and space. Gold jewelry, like a necklace or earrings, has different names and forms, but the essence is gold. The waves in an ocean are analogous to creation in the cosmic ocean of God's consciousness. Although the waves in an ocean swell up then break and seem to disappear, they still remain as the ocean at all times. All creation is connected with the invisible common thread of God consciousness.

- The entire universe is one family.
- God (universal consciousness) is our father.
- Goddess (God's energy or prakriti) is our mother.
- The earth is our root
- The sky is our roof.
- The four directions are the walls.
- We are all children of eternity.
- I am grateful to God for all the gifts of life.
- I am grateful to all my ancestors, parents, teachers, society, nature and myself.
- I forgive all the beings that may have offended me knowingly or unknowingly in the past.
- I pray for the health, harmony and peace of all beings.
- I love my family of diversity.
- Everyone is evolving at his or her own rate. I love them with compassion as they are.
- I feel the security and protection of my divine father and mother.
- I feel the friendship of my family members.

- I am surrounded by love, peace and abundance.
- I feel the joy of living and flourish in the comfort of the harmonious universe.
- I feel content.

## 5. ACTIVE MEDITATION PRACTICE

Active meditation is applied during the day while performing activities. Observe the breath during the day and let it become slow and rhythmic. Let it becomes a habit. Your eyes can remain open. No one will be able to tell what you are doing. You can practice while walking, driving or washing dishes. Breathing will remain slow and rhythmic. Lots of mental energy is wasted during the day with chattering mind. It will stop the drainage of energy and will revive you. Ultimately you remain aware of your breath while talking or interacting with others.

As you advance, try to be an observer standing outside of your body. Instead of saying "I am hungry," you say "My stomach is hungry." You create separation from your body, senses and mind. You become observer of your movements, speech and actions. Being an observer, you become non-judgmental. You break the pattern of compulsive behavior of reacting or over reacting. You become visionary and act constructively.

You can break compulsive habits of eating, smoking, worries or anger. By being an observer you slow down the process. For compulsive eating, feel desire to eat, feel the touch of food, smell of food, hand approaching the mouth, feeling in the mouth. Slowing down the process removes programmed behavior. It is similar to policemen catching a thief by looking at video camera in slow motion, enlarging or freezing the picture.

One uses life and situations in life as a school to learn spiritual lessons. One uses selfless service to expand consciousness. One experiences universality with all living creatures. One sees that all creation is interconnected like beads in a garland with a common thread of supreme consciousness. Everyone is like a wave in the cosmic ocean of life. One experiences his own existence as the ocean instead of an individual wave. The individual wave has a beginning and an end, while the universal ocean is immortal (Sat), consciousness (Chit) and bliss (Anand). One harmonizes his or her own life to remain in rhythm with the universe. The acts we perform to remain in rhythm are called Dharma or the universal law. Dharma is the way for personal and universal transformation.

## 6. GUIDELINES FOR MATERIAL AND SPIRITUAL SUCCESS

Material and spiritual paths require same disciplines. The difference is material path is directed towards the world while spiritual path is directed towards the Self. One who knows how to be successful in the world also knows the tools to be successful in spiritual life. One just needs to turn around and take direction towards the Self.

Success requires energy. If a speedy car is going in the wrong direction, it can turn around and recover lost distance easily.

A person who cannot succeed in the world cannot succeed in the spiritual life. World is a school and spiritual life is college. One has to experience the world and find contentment so worldly attractions drop away. Then one can enter the college of spiritual life.

Many people renounce the world prematurely and become monks. They are escapists. Their attachments to world can take perverted forms.

Success comes by learning to manage energy, money and time. One can attain wealth by accumulating small amounts of money over time. One earns time by being continually efficient. One preserves energy by restraining physical and mental activities. "Time and tide wait for no one" and "make hay while the sun shines" are old sayings that carry the basic message. Utilize all opportunities efficiently. Following are general guidelines for success.

- Clarity: Attain clarity of goal and direction. Change means as necessary.
- Love: Cultivate love for your goal.
- Decision: Take time to choose direction in life. Stay on the path. A wavering mind oscillates like a pendulum and drains energy.
- Commitment: Take responsibility and be committed to

practice. Give up dependency on others.

- Priority: Set priorities and be willing to sacrifice.
- Urgency: Create urgency as if you have only a short time to live
- Intensity: Add power to your practice by focusing with intensity.
- Creative Energy: Think outside the box, cultivate intuition. Avoid lethargy, laziness and procrastination, and create new personal path to success.
- Enthusiasm: Seek constant Satsang for inspiration and to sustain enthusiasm.
- Inspiration: Get recharged with stillness, meditation and introspection.
- Patience and Perseverance: Be committed to practice without expectation of results.
- Undercurrent: Sustain undercurrent of interest in your goal so it penetrates all levels of your consciousness. Integrate positive affirmations in your life.
- Surrender: After applying above principles, just relax. Surrender the fruits of your actions action to God. Remove the burden of doership. Expand consciousness. Tune into universal consciousness for guidance and support.

# PART 3: SPIRITUAL REFLECTIONS

## ACCEPTANCE

Acceptance does not mean being lazy, merely putting up with difficult situations, or escaping reality. Acceptance is getting to know your body, mind, emotions, talents, aptitude and overall personality. Make peace instead of fighting yourself. Acceptance means exploring and using your inner potential instead of looking outside for solutions. It is like a person who has hidden treasure in the cellar of the house but lives and dies in poverty without ever discovering it.

Accept old age, sickness, diseases, accidents and death as realities of life. Consider life as a privilege and flow with life instead of taking everything for granted. Remember the prayer of serenity: "God grant me serenity to accept the things I cannot change, courage to change the things I can and wisdom to know the difference."

By looking outside, one gets in competition with others or becomes jealous of others. Grass always looks greener from a distance. Acceptance means looking in the mirror and letting go of illusions about yourself so that you can deal with real issues of life. Acceptance is the starting point of your life's journey to success. One enjoys the journey being in the moment and flows with life, instead of worrying about the results.

## ALONENESS AND LONELINESS

Aloneness and loneliness are on the opposite ends of each other.

When you connect with Atman or higher Self, you expand consciousness and feel unity with entire universe. This is called aloneness. You remain in the present and there is no one but you. There is no one to impress or to fear. You remain comfortable being alone or in a crowd.

When you are disconnected from Self, you feel lonely. You produce duality of you and I. You feel isolated and threatened by the world. Duality is the cause of fears and worries. Crowds and activities cannot remove your loneliness. Aloneness means removing external stimulations and being content within your Self. One should cultivate friendship with Self frequently with meditation and constant awareness. Self will become your support and dependence on others will diminish.

## APPRECIATION

We have general tendency to go outward instead of looking within. Grass always looks greener at a distance. Such illusions guide the life of masses. They remain busy running outside and do not think of looking within. They focus on what is lacking in their imagination and forget to appreciate all the beauty of nature and gifts of God. If we change our vision, we can be instantaneously happy under all circumstances.

We can survive without food for months, and survive without water for days but cannot survive without air for more than a few minutes. Yet we take breathing for granted and do not pay attention to it. We ignore the teachers and teachings in front of us and run for them outside. We pay premium price for things that are more expensive and inaccessible and ignore the things available for free in front of us. We do not appreciate masters when they are alive and worship them after they are gone. We do not appreciate Self (Atman) within, which is the source of bliss and wisdom and search for happiness in the world.

## AUM

Aum is the symbol that represents supreme consciousness or Brahman. It is presented on the top of the chart in this book, with its three qualities of Sat, chit and Anand. Entire universe is nothing but vibrations. Scientists found that vibration of entire universe is Aum. Aum is the eternal sound of silence.

- A is the starting point of sound and comes from inner depth. It can be uttered without use of tongue, teeth or lips. Even a dumb person and animals can say it. It represents waking state of consciousness (Jagrat), balance state of nature (Satva) and past tense of time. It represents eternal existence (Sat).
- U is the middle of sound, and covers all ranges of sound. It represents dream state of consciousness (Swapna), activity mode of nature (Rajas), and present state of time. It represents consciousness (Chit).
- M is the end of sound. It can be uttered with lips closed. It represents deep sleep state of consciousness (Susupti), inertia mode of nature (Tamas) and future tense of time. It represents bliss (Anand).
- AUM is the total combination of the three sounds. It transcends the three states of consciousness and modes of nature and time. One can chant Aum aloud properly, to synchronize vibrations in the body. Then tunes into subtle vibrations of Aum to transcend the mind, and experience Atman/Brahman.

## AUSTERITY (TAPAS)

Austerities (Tapas) mean facing hardship. It takes effort to reach the top of a hill. Accomplishments require some effort. In applying austerity one has to resist temptations and comforts. This purifies the mind and builds will power. One chooses disciplines with clarity of purpose. An Olympic athlete makes various sacrifices willingly and practices regularly without complaints. His goal motivates him. A laborer does heavy work compulsively to survive. He has no choice. This is not austerity.

Tapas also mean heating. Gold is purified by heating. In the same way, mind is made pure by the heat of austerity.

Following disciplines to achieve a spiritual goal with a smiling face for self-purification is called Satvik Austerity. It leads to liberation. Torturing body or mind due to ignorance of purpose is called Tamasik austerity. It is destructive. Performing austerities for recognition or reward in the future is called Rajasik austerity. It binds us to law of Karma. Most spiritual austerities such as fasting and giving up pleasures are for the purpose of restraining the senses and the mind to achieve peace and purity.

## AVIDYA (IGNORANCE)

Spiritual knowledge is called Vidya. It liberates one. All other knowledge is called Avidya. Avidya means spiritual blindness. One does not perceive the ultimate reality. One considers impermanent as permanent, pain as pleasure, impure as pure and non-Self as Self. This becomes the cause of bondage and suffering.

When one experiences the world subjectively, with the intent of knowing the purpose of life, this is called Vidya. One explores the world objectively to find temporary happiness or comforts, this is called Avidya.

One can be a scholar in worldly matters, but lack Self-knowledge and suffer in life. Worldly knowledge may help in earning money and building a career but it does not give peace. On the other hand, one can be illiterate but possess Self-knowledge and experience lasting peace. Many uneducated spiritual masters became awakened and experienced the essence of the scriptures. They provided guidance and peace to monks, pundits, and masses of people.

## AWARENESS (JAGRUTI)

Intellect along with I-Consciousness produces awareness. Consciousness is like a sharp tool that penetrates the experience using awareness. Awareness transforms life instantaneously. It allows us to make a quantum leap toward experience of Self.

Awareness involves vigilance and alertness in observing and gaining firsthand knowledge, intense concentration and intuitive perception. All these steps happen simultaneously and transform life. One can cultivate effortless awareness to become a witness of body, senses, mind and emotions and become free from slavery to them.

We have the choice to remain asleep or awaken to awareness. With awareness pleasant and unpleasant experiences of life become means of awakening. One uses comforts efficiently with gratitude and treats problems as challenges to be faced rather than escaped.

Awareness is the awakened state of spiritual evolution. Wise people are awake to higher Self and asleep to worldly pursuits, while ignorant people are awake to worldly ambitions and asleep to the higher Self.

## BALANCE AND SURPLUS
We need to balance our thoughts and emotions, our personal life and social life, and rest and physical and mental activities

We need to manage money, time and energy by balancing them. They can buy each other. For example, with proper management of money, you can buy the time needed to nurture your body with diet and exercises. With mismanagement of money, you can waste time and indulge in wrong habits.

We have limited supply of time, money and energy. One third of life is spent sleeping. The remainder is spent surviving, engaging in social activities and seeking pleasure. Most people have fixed income and a limited supply of energy.

The main source of stress comes from shortage of money, time or energy. One should create surplus and be prepared for emergency. Surplus will give you peace of mind and freedom to meditate and realize Self.

We can create surplus through clarity of goal and awareness. One can set priority as if there is limited time to live. We plan for years ahead as if we are immortal while in reality we have no guarantee of tomorrow. We can cultivate efficiency and make necessary sacrifices to prioritize what really matters in life. We can maintain an undercurrent of awareness of our goal for Self-knowledge. This will serve as a constant reminder and provide inspiration on the journey.

## BLISS (ANAND), HAPPINESS (SUKHA), PLEASURE AND ILLUSIVE PLEASURE
Bliss is our essential nature. It is the constant source of happiness. Happiness is its reflection. Pleasure and illusive pleasure are further reflections. Bliss is like sun; its reflection on earth is like happiness. Earth's reflection on moon is like pleasure. When we interact with our loved ones, we become introverted and get in touch with Self and feel happiness. This generates love in the heart and involves flow of Prana. It is the direct reflection of bliss and

takes us closer to the Self. It feels like happiness came from loved ones and we get attached. But Self is actual source.

When we experience pleasure of the senses, we become introverted and feel like pleasure came from outside. It is the diluted reflection of bliss. For example: when we get involved in eating and experience aha!! Moment, we become introverted and get in touch with Self. Subject, object and the process become one. We experience bliss for a moment and feel pleasure came from the food. One repeats the process due to this illusion. All sense pleasures are secondary reflections of bliss.

Experiencing sense pleasure drains our vital energy. A dog chewing on a bone feels pleasure came from the bone. In reality it comes from own bleeding gums. End product of pleasure is pain but we do not see it due to ignorance.

When we think about our possessions or fame, we become introverted in a daydream and feel illusion of pleasure. It is the faintest reflection of bliss. It is less tangible and temporary. If the world does not recognize your name or the possessions you have accumulated, it gives pain.

When we become aware, we realize that bliss is our basic nature. We stop running outward and focus within to attain long lasting bliss.

## CELIBACY (BRAHMACHARYA)
Brahman means God or Self. Directing energy towards Self is Brahmacharya. One gets occupied with spiritual disciplines and selfless service and attraction to pleasure of senses drops away naturally. Brahmacharya is generally interpreted as giving up sex by condemning sex. Sexual energy is gift of God that sustains creation. It is the highest source of energy available for creativity and spiritual evolution. Sexual energy cannot be suppressed by force. It would only take perverted form. Simplicity of diet, abstaining from sense stimulation, meditation and selfless service helps restraining sexual energy. Sexual energy can be sublimated into spiritual energy or aura (Ojas), or converted to other creative manifestations. Aura is the invisible subtle part of our existence which speaks louder than our speech or body language.

## CENTER OF THE UNIVERSE (SELF)

We are Self (Atman) at the center of the universe. World revolves around us. We are the subject and world is the object. We can exist without the world, but world cannot exist without us. Self is like a number and world is like zeros. Zeros have no value without a number in front. Center of wheel remains steady while circumference rotates constantly. If we realize this, we become master of our life. We are the co-creator of our destiny. We are the starting point of all actions. World is reflection of our being. If we love others, it creates feeling of love within us before reaching others. If we feel anger or hate, it affects us before reaching others.

People suffer because they give more importance to the world, attach to it and are controlled by the world and forget their own Self is the master.

People cannot get along with others in the world because they have not learnt to get along with themselves.

## CHARITY (DANA)

Most religions recommend giving certain portion of income as charity. It is our natural duty to share instead of hoarding. Stagnant waters become dirty and flowing waters remain pure. We become instrumental in receiving and giving. Hoarding is the root cause of psychosomatic problems just like constipation is the root cause of health problem.

Charity begins at home. First nurture yourself before serving others. One needs surplus to give charity. You can give money if you have surplus of it. You can give a helping hand if you have surplus of time and energy. A beggar cannot give charity.

Satvik charity is given to the right recipient at right time and right place with love and compassion. It expands our consciousness and reduces our ego and attachments. Charity gets wasted if it is given indiscriminately. When charity is given with expectation or recognition, it is Rajasik charity and builds attachments. When one gives charity unwillingly with anger is Tamasik charity which binds one.

Giving financial help is superficial charity that does not last. Giving education is a longer lasting charity. Giving spiritual guidance is the longest lasting charity that transforms life.

You can help someone whom you know in some capacity

instead giving to a popular charity where only a small portion reaches the recipient. If you have nothing to offer as charity, you can smile or say a few sweet words to spread joy. You can pray for well-being of others. You can remain silent and spread peace through your presence.

## CHITTA (UNCONSCIOUS MIND)

Chitta is innermost hidden part of the mind. It is like the hidden part of an iceberg. Conscious mind is only the visible part of mind. Chitta stores the impressions of current life and previous lives. It is like recording device. It receives information from external sources. It does not think but follows commands. These impressions are called Sanskaras. Chitta stores impressions depending upon intensity of attachment and also through constant bombardment of information. Unconscious mind is more receptive during relaxation. Growing years are more valuable years to program chitta than during college education.

Sanskaras are the undercurrent that regulates our life, using imprinted conditions and inner programming. Logic or harsh physical and mental disciplines or religious indoctrination have no power over Sanskaras. They can be removed through regression with awareness or deep affirmations and meditation.

Mind follows five kinds of wave patterns (Chitta vritti) during waking, dreaming and deep sleep. When one controls them and connects with Self (Atman), he attains Self-Realization.

## CHOICES

We have choices in life in all situations. If we are not aware to choose, we will be slave to circumstances. If we listen to others or try to please others, we become their slaves. They control our life and happiness. If we listen to our senses, they lead us to more sensations and short-term pleasure. We become slaves of our desires. If we listen to our higher Self, It leads to wisdom and liberates us.

We have choice to be happy or unhappy. Happiness is the state of mind. We do not have control over our situations of life, but we always have control over our mind. Even people who lack health, wealth and opportunities can choose to be happy. If you have wisdom, you can be happy in any situation. Some people choose to be unhappy despite abundance of everything.

We have choice to choose direction in life. There is an ongoing tug of war between the world and Self. When attraction to the world diminishes due to renunciation, and attraction to the Self increases with desire for liberation, one succeeds on the spiritual path.

We have choice to magnify faults of others and minimize our own faults, or magnify our faults to purify ourselves and minimize faults of others to forgive them.

We can choose superficial friends who flatter us for some gain or real friends who criticize us to benefit us.

## CONTENTMENT (SANTOSH)

One who is satisfied becomes content. People with inner poverty usually run after wealth. People with inner insecurity usually run for power or fame.

Contentment is not laziness. Both look similar on the surface. A lazy person wants success to fall in his lap. A fox who is too lazy to reach for the grapes declares that grapes are sour anyway. A content person does not want anything even if it offered.

Contentment is like a saturated sponge that cannot absorb any more water. Those who find inner peace of Self become saturated and content. They stop running and remain immune to the temptations of the world.

When one attains wisdom, attachments drop naturally just like leaves fall effortlessly in the autumn, and renunciation happens. Whole world becomes home. Contentment is the climax of happiness. Contentment is superior to excitement and pleasure. Excitement disturbs hunger, sleep and peace of mind. Contentment is ideal for creativity, healing and meditation.

## CONVERSION AND TRANSFORMATION

Masses of people get converted by following blindly. Conversion means adding on layers of illusion to hide the truth of Self. It is due to insecurity and need to protect ego. One needs constant push from outside.

Most religious and spiritual leaders focus on converting people. Young people and people with low self-esteem become victims of conversion. Masses of people get mesmerized in a large crowd by indoctrination. Their conversion only builds ego instead of changing their lives. They follow mechanical practices, change names, clothes and life style that gives them identity and security. They feel greater security by converting others.

For transformation, one has to be self-reliant, think and question instead follow blindly. One has to hatch out of the egg of conditioning and be reborn like birds of flight.

Transformation is an inside out process like a blooming of a flower or a seed turning into a plant. One has to let go of old identity. It is a personal, lonely journey. One thinks, questions and experiments. One takes responsibility of own life and remains grounded on personal convictions. Transformation is an effortless unfolding process. It flows with life and is creative. Transformation is self sustained and does not need outside push.

## DEATH (MRITYU)
We exist as body, senses, mind, intellect and consciousness. Prana sustains our life. When prana departs the body, heart, lungs and nerve impulse stop working and body starts decaying. This is called death.

At the time of death, matter of body returns back to the earth and prana returns to universal prana. Soul (Jivatma) continues the journey and chooses appropriate body to fulfill deep desires. Jivatma means pure Atman contaminated with sanskaras in Chitta.

Jivatma carries all the Sanskaras of past lives just like wind carries odors and fragrances. Sanskaras have energy to manifest appropriate body. We cannot fool Mother Nature. Law of Karma is precise and there are no exceptions. What we sow, so we reap.

Death is like a longer dream. After waking up we continue with next day, same way soul continues the journey with fresh enthusiasm.

Death means changing the bodies like changing clothes. We choose appropriate body to fulfill our desires. After birth, we get covered up with influence of Maya and forget our past lives. However, experiences are hidden in the Chitta. Past experiences come on the surface and past talents revive. One retains free will which pushes one to continue journey.

Atman is immortal and is not subject to birth or death. God has created built in power so that all living creatures have fear of death

(Abhinivesha) and try to protect and preserve own life. When one wakes up from Maya, the cosmic dream ends. A wave merges in the ocean. It ends the process of birth and death and transmigration.

## DESIRES (VAASANA)

There are normal desires which are healthy. Desires for survival and success in life should not be condemned. One should cultivate talents such as arts, music, athletics, or writing. They can be means of meditation. Desires become dangerous when one looks for recognition and reward.

Desires for running after and gratifying pleasure are dangerous. This intense desire is called craving (Tanaha). Craving makes one blind. Cravings are the root cause of all evils. Desires cannot be fulfilled. Fulfilling desires is like pouring gasoline on fire. Desires produce chain reaction of greed, false ego, attachment and hatred. Desires ultimately get interrupted and cause anger. Desires are the root cause of transmigration. These six vices (Shad ripus) are considered enemies of spiritual life.

Desire for liberation is the only desire that can liberate us. One should use all other desires to support this main desire. Other desires tie us to the pleasure of the world and bind us to transmigration.

## DESTINY (PRARABDHA)

Destiny is considered as fate. It suggests pre-determined course of events beyond our powers. In reality, there are laws of Karma that determines outcome in precise manner. We are the co-creator of our destiny. Since we do not see the hidden aspects of Karma, we believe that we are controlled by destiny.

Karmas of the past and past lives are stored in the unconscious mind. When these ripen suddenly in the present life, unexpected gain or loss occurs. This is called destiny or Prarbdha. It is similar to fixed deposit account that gives lump sum gain at the maturity. We are responsible for our destiny but cannot see it.

We have control over our actions but have very little control over the outcome. Outcome is determined by our destiny. Other people or situations become instrumental in determining the outcome. We become a victim of an accident because of someone else's fault. Everyone and everything is interconnected in the universe beyond boundaries of time and influence each other. Collective Karmas can become destiny for groups of people and can result as collective disaster. Because of Prarabdha, we choose appropriate parent and environments. We can be at a wrong place and wrong time to be a victim of disaster or at a proper time and space to be lucky. Sometimes we make decisions due to influence of Prarabdha that can cause gain or loss. During Samadhi, one can remove Sanskaras of past lives and can change one's destiny.

## DEVOTION TO GOD (BHAKTI)

Bhakti means constant remembrance of God or intense love for God. One loves all and hates none. One can remember God with each breath as ceaseless prayer. One becomes satisfied. Bhakti is the means and Bhakti is the goal for the devotee. This path is called Bhakti Yoga.

Most people know conditional love. Bhakti is unconditional love for God and his creation. Bhakti can be cultivated by nine steps of devotional practices (Navadha bhakti). It involves worshipping the image of chosen deity by various rituals to cultivate attachment to deity and detachment from the world. Most people get lost in the rituals.

Human love is conditional love, yet gives us opportunity to cultivate unconditional love. We love others unconditionally and accept them as they are without expecting anything in return. We can cultivate unconditional love with family, friends and other human beings. When Bhakti matures, one attains supreme love for all living creature and is called Para Bhakti. Bhakti is born when one is amazed by the mysterious creation of the creator and has desire to meet the creator. His heart gets saturated with love and compassion.

## DHARMA

Dharma sustains entire universe. All natural forces like sun, moon, ocean etc. follow their Dharma. They give unconditionally. To remain healthy and happy, one has to remain in tune with universal rhythm and flow with life. Animals follow nature's rhythm due to instinct. Humans use intellect and go against the rhythm of nature and suffer. Religions established Ten Commandments and yoga has ten rules of yamas and niyamas to guide people on the moral path of Dharma. One should follow moral discipline in the appropriate spirit, so that it is in line with Dharma and produces harmony.

There are Dharmas connected with age, stage of life, profession, relationship and one's spiritual development. We are indebted to our ancestors, teachers, country and nature. We have natural Dharma to worship and respect elders, teachers, sun, moon, rivers, mountains, trees, animals and all creations of God. We should use natural resources with gratitude and not pollute them. We should learn to give unconditionally like nature.

Dharma brings health and happiness in life. Many physical and psychological diseases are created by going against Dharma. Dharma is the foundation and fundamental support for spiritual life. When religious morality is practiced literally instead of in its proper spirit, it becomes destructive. Dharma is not rigid. It is determined by intuition. It is dynamic and changes with time and situation.

## DO NOT JUDGE OTHERS
We have no capacity to judge others. If we judge by their looks, clothing, speech or actions, it will mislead us. Try to feel their vibrations without using the mind. Judgment produces prejudices and prevents us from experiencing reality.

We judge others at our level of consciousness. We rely on our past experiences in judging others. We project our limited reality and confine ourselves. Those who are in line with us are considered friends and against us are called enemies. Everyone has some unique talents and gifts. Discover them and learn from them. Minimize the faults of others and magnify their virtues. One should experience life fully with a fresh eye, as if seeing it for the first time. Use freshness in all relations, activities and possessions to find joy and inspiration in life. Without freshness, life becomes boring. Excitement of a new car, lottery or new house and loved ones diminishes quickly unless we see with fresh eyes every day.

Accept everyone as a spark of divine in human body or animal body. Accept everyone as they are. They are at a different stage of evolution. A tomato plant cannot be an oak tree. This attitude gives us compassion to forgive them. Do not judge others from your past interaction with them. There is great possibility that they have changed over years and you have changed as well.

## DOING AND UNDOING (KARMA AND AKARMA)

All living creatures are vibrating energy. Life cannot exist without performing some activities. Three modes (Gunas) of nature ( Prakriti) compel all living creatures to act. Breathing and heart beats are involuntary activities of all creatures. All actions bring reaction and bind us. Trying to stop activity is also an activity. The only way to become free from activities is to remove the identity of being a doer by realizing that all actions are done by nature (Gunas). We can perform our duty (Dharma) using our faculties as an instrument of God and remain as an observer. This awareness turns doing into undoing and frees us from bondage.

We use our body, senses and mind for performing any activity. All actions produce reaction. This is called "Law of karma." One becomes a doer and becomes responsible for all actions and produces Karma. Actions of mind produce deeper impact than speech and action. For performing our Dharma we may hurt some people and still we may be free from Karma because we have no intention of hurting anyone. On the other hand thinking of hurting someone without physically hurting them can produce Karma. We produce Karma with our intention and intensity that registers in the unconscious mind (Chitta).

Doing builds stress while undoing removes all burdens. Undoing is like letting go to tune into God consciousness. We experience divine energy.

Undoing means using body senses and mind as instrument of God and remaining relaxed as a witness. This is practice of "Karma Yoga" that turns actions into inaction. Realize that we are not the doers (Karta) or enjoyer (Bokta) but an observer or witness (Drishta).

## DUALITY (DWAITA)

Duality means two. When pure consciousness identifies itself with body, senses or mind, it produces ego or dichotomy of subject and object. I becomes subject and world becomes object. Pleasure/pain, gain/loss, heat/cold, honor/insult, success/failure are products of duality and cause of our suffering. They are like two sides of a coin. One is hidden within the other.

Duality produces feeling of you and I. It is the cause of fears, anger and loneliness. Duality shrinks our consciousness and produces divisions. It is the cause of wars of nations, family feuds and personal conflicts. If duality is reduced, one feels unity of life and world feels like extension of own being.

Spiritual awakening means to remove duality and feel unity of life (Advaita). One remains as an observer and is not touched by dualities in life. One remains at the center of the wheel of life while the world revolves around him. There are four eternal sayings (Maha Vakyas) of Advaita philosophy is "So Hum" or "I am that," is one of the essential mantras of Advaita.

## DYNAMIC FAITH (SHRADDHA)

Faith is not just belief, or belonging to any faith, or joining any religion. Most people use faith as an escape. They belong to some religion or follow dogma, waiting for miracles instead of taking charge of their own life. They feel comfortable only in the cocoon of familiar environments and are threatened by different cultures, beliefs or faiths. They waste energy defending themselves or converting others to their beliefs to build their ego. They become annoyed and irritated facing adverse situations in life instead of flowing with life.

Many people consider themselves as devout followers of their religion, follow rigid disciplines, pray frequently and surrender to God. Yet they suffer from stress, insomnia, worries and depressions. This clearly shows their immaturity in faith.

Blind faith is an escape. It gives temporary relief while hiding insecurities and doubts. A non believer has greater chance of evolution than a blind follower. He takes responsibility for his life and has a chance to wake up.

Faith can be cultivated by using logic, contemplation, meditation, and application until it becomes your personal conviction and gives you guidance and support. You become compassionate for all creatures and all people regardless of their looks or beliefs.

## EFFORT AND GRACE (KRIPA)

If one relies only on effort, he will be exhausted and feel stress. If one waits for grace, it will be an escape. We have to rely on effort and then patiently wait for grace and accept result.

Karma yoga teaches one to perform your Dharma and give up desires for reward. Surrender the outcome to God and accept the outcome as blessings (Prasad) with love.

We have control over our actions but results depend upon external factors of environment, other beings, and situations, and our stored karmas of the past (Prarabdha).

God's grace showers on everyone at all times. We have to keep up with constant effort to catch it. One has to get the garden ready to utilize rain instead of digging garden when the rain arrives. Time and tide wait for none. We receive inspiration during prayers and meditation. We should consider inspiration as a message of God and act on it instead of sitting and waiting for God to save you. A rescue squad helps only those who are on the roof during the flood. God helps those who help themselves to their capacity and surrender for rescue.

## EGO (AHANKAR)

I-Consciousness is called Ahankar. It is the consciousness which observes everything without judgment or involvement. It is the meditative state. When consciousness attaches itself with body, senses, mind or emotions, it is called ego.

Ego produces duality of you and I and causes problems. Ego is energy and manifests and is expressed by three modes (Gunas) of nature. At Tamasik state ego is dormant. One is content due to ignorance. It is the bliss of ignorance. One wants pleasures but is too lazy to get it. It is like a fox that says "Grapes are sour" because he cannot reach up the vine. In Rajasik state, ego is active earning wealth, and seeking pleasure and power. It produces restlessness and discontentment. While in Satvik state, ego produces contentment. Satvik state is ideal for spiritual evolution. Highest evolution is Gunatit state, which transcends three states of nature (Gunas) and allows one to become free. In the earlier stages of evolution, one has to build ego as self-confidence. In advanced stages, one cultivates compassion and ego drops away. One has to evolve from Tamasik state to Satvik state for spiritual evolution.

If one slaps you on one cheek, you hold other cheek if you are a coward (insufficient ego). Or you may slap back if you have enough strength to defeat the other party (stronger ego enables survival). But in advanced stage, one consciously forgives due to real strength and compassion (one transcends ego). In Tamasik state one is like a jelly fish without energy. In Rajasik state one has energy for personal gain and success. In Satvik state one has balance and compassion to serve others. First build ego and then kill it. Ego is used to kill the ego. A thorn is used to pick other thorn, and then both thorns are thrown away.

## ENERGY AND CONSCIOUSNESS (PRANA AND CHETNA)

Entire universe is nothing but combination of consciousness (Purusha) and energy (Prakriti). Consciousness means built in intelligence that directs energy. Prana means subtlest unit of energy which pervades entire universe. Both Purusha and Prakriti are eternal and beyond boundaries. All sentient and insentient beings are part of Consciousness and Energy. Minerals are the lowest form and humans are the highest form of expression.

- Laziness: Laziness is the lack of energy. It is like a car out of gas.
- Restlessness: Restlessness is uncontrolled energy. A running car with a drunk driver. There is no direction and it is destructive.
- Relaxation: Mind is alert and energy is available. It is like car running in neutral gear. A cat sits quietly and attacks a mouse at the right time.
- I-Consciousness (Ahankar): It is the pure sense of "I Am" without any adjuncts. It is the witness without involvement.
- Ego: When I-Conscious identifies itself with body, senses or mind and becomes one with it.
- Dreams: Consciousness is disconnected from the body. Mind works with memories and fantasies without the use of the body.
- Deep sleep: Consciousness is disconnected from body and mind. There is absence of experience and absence of sense of time until one wakes up. Just like a person during anesthetic influence.

- Deep Meditation: Consciousness is disconnected from body and connected to Supreme Consciousness. Transformation takes place.
- Transcendental state: Deep Samadhi. Individual consciousness merges with universal consciousness. Wave dissolves and becomes ocean. One transcends all limitations of time and space. One attains true wisdom during Samadhi.

## ENVIRONMENT

Environment influences our life. Our senses and unconscious mind get influenced by environment. We are influenced by colors, sounds, smell, touch and taste. Feng Shui and Vastu are sciences that focus on proper environments for the home for harmony and peace.

Experiments have proven that water crystals react to environment. Healing environment produces perfect crystals while disturbing environment forms distorted crystals. We are mostly made of water and get influenced by environment. Plants flourish with loving care and Aum vibrations. Genetic scientists have proven that our genes can mutate by changing environment.

We should choose company of holy persons and avoid company of evil persons. Their influence of thinking, talking and behavior rubs off on us gradually. If you go to a coal mine with white clothes, they get stained even if you are careful. We have choice to create healing environment in the meditation room and at home. Home and meditation room should be sanctuary for healing. One should spend money building a meditation room in the house instead of spending money to decorate house to impress others. One should choose a lesser paying job which produces healing environment above a high paying job that is stressful.

## FASTING (OOPVAS)

Fasting is a spiritual discipline common to all religions and cultures. Fasting is called Oopvas. Oop means closer and Vas means living. Oopvas means staying closer to God. Fasting is abstaining from food. Food nourishes body. Body is the field that supports senses, mind and intellect. Supreme Consciousness has become a prisoner of the body. It is confined by senses and the mind. By fasting, one removes the stronghold of senses and mind and establishes closer contact with Consciousness. It quiets the mind and deepens meditation. True fasting is resting five sense organs, five motor organs and the mind. Many spiritual masters followed fasting and meditation in seclusion for spiritual awakening.

Fasting is the best means of resting and healing the body. It provides rest to digestion and all related organs and the mind. It promotes cleansing process to remove toxins from the body and revives it. It is the scientific method to remove diseases. Purified body becomes a temple to invite God.

One should learn the science of fasting before approaching fasting. Ideal fast is water fast. Common guidance for fasting is fasting on daily basis by eating less than hunger, eating only when hungry. Set a day for fasting, observing silence, resting and meditation.

Fasting is a science and most religions have introduced it as spiritual discipline. Most people follow fasting mechanically as rigid discipline without understanding and damage themselves. They practice it as ritual and festivity. They stop fasting with sudden overeating or allow the consumption of substitute foods that are damaging.

## FLOW WITH LIFE

Life is like a rough ocean. We need to get along with life instead of fighting it. We need to cultivate renunciation to keep afloat in life. If we learn to swim, we can swim whether the water is shallow or deep. Getting along with the world requires learning to get along with ourselves.

Yogi Patanjali gives advice on how to get along with other people. There are four kinds of people in the world. 1. Happy people (Sukhi). Be friends with them and share their joy instead of being jealous. 2. Unhappy people (Dukhi). Cultivate compassion instead of criticizing or hating them. 3. Virtuous people (Punyatma). Enjoy their company and receive inspiration from them. 4. Wicked people (Papatma). Avoid them when possible or be indifferent to them.

Life is universal flow. You cannot fight it. When you sail a boat, you flow with waves, currents and wind. When you practice yoga positions, allow prana to flow and regulate movements instead forcing your body or mind. When you flow with life, you find effortless success and peace of mind.

## FORGIVENESS (KSHAMA)

All experiences leave impression in the unconscious mind (Chitta). We especially register experiences which produce strong likes and dislikes. We have subtle anger and resentment for people who have offended us in the past. We hold unconscious anger for them. Sometimes we blame ourselves for past mistakes. Forgiveness produces instant relief from burdens. It removes Sanskara before they grow deeper roots in the unconscious mind.

Forgiving others becomes easier if we cultivate compassion for them. We can have compassion if we try to understand their situation. We should accept everyone as they are. They are at their own level of evolution. Tomato plant and an oak tree are both plants, but at different levels. We accept babies when they do not talk and forgive a blind person if he bumps into us. Our resistance comes from expectation. We accept when a stranger betrays us but cannot tolerate loved one betraying us. Holding a grudge against anyone only disturbs our peace.

We should learn to forgive others and ourselves. Deep-rooted rage produces diseases in the body and hinders our present life. It is the cause of destructive behaviors like road rage, which hurt others and us. Forgiveness will free our mind to experience deeper peace.

## FREEDOM AND DISCIPLINE

Freedom is the result of discipline. Freedom without discipline is dangerous. Speed of a car without discipline of brakes and steering is dangerous. Discipline enables a musician to produce music instead of noise.

We search for political, economic and social freedom. These freedoms are of secondary nature. Real freedom comes when we become liberated from the conditioning of the mind and become our own master. Mind is the cause of freedom and bondage.

One needs to dam the river and build reservoir to provide water and energy. Discipline of time builds reservoir to give surplus and freedom of time. Discipline of money gives freedom of money and discipline of energy gives freedom for activities.

When one follows disciplines with love, it becomes self sustained. It becomes effortless lifestyle. One gives up destructive habits that hurt our body and mind.

## GIVING AND RECEIVING

Joy is doubled by sharing. According to Bhagavad Gita, Those who eat alone (who do not share) are eating sin. It means they suffer by being self centered. Hoarding is produced by insecurity and leads to fear, shrinking consciousness, and psychosomatic diseases. Just like water remains clean when it is flowing, sharing purifies the heart.

Receiving should be done selectively. Receiving can produce obligations and expectation from the giver. Sometimes people reciprocate favors in conflict with moral laws. For example, lobbyists give donation to politicians with expectation of receiving a favor. One of the Yamas (Moral code) of Raja yoga is Aprigraha. It means one should not be greedy and not accept favors. This way one does not have to deviate from the path in returning favors.

One should give and receive unconditionally. Giving or receiving conditionally ties us to the law of Karma and causes suffering. Religious holidays have turned into commercial businesses. People waste time in giving and receiving gifts with expectations and feel stress instead of joy. Real gift is to get together and share joy of holidays instead of focusing on exchanging of gifts.

## GRATITUDE

We should learn to be grateful for all the gifts of life. We should be grateful for healthy body, food, shelter, clothing and loving family and friends. How much are we willing spend to save eyes or limbs? If we count the value of each faculty we have, we will be filled with gratitude. When we think of the supreme power that carries on functions of heart, lungs, digestion and healing without effort, we will be filled with gratitude.

Ancient Vedas have hymns and symbolic offerings for worshipping sun, fire, air, earth, and water as demigods (Devas). These are gestures of gratitude that attune us to God. When chanted properly, these prayers can transform a person. Gratitude will saturate us with love and appreciation for God. We learn to praise the Lord instead of complain about what we lack. It will prevent us from wrong desires, competition, comparison and jealousy.

Some people count the blessings of God and become content. Some people complain about what they lack and become miserable.

## GROSS AND SUBTLE (STHOOL AND SUKSHMA)

Entire universe is made of five rudimentary elements called Panch Maha Bhutas. They are space, air, fire, water and earth. Space is the subtlest eternal and all pervasive background. It projects air, fire, and water and earth elements from subtle to gross. Entire universe reflects similar pattern.

- Subtle is invisible while gross is visible.
- Subtle is more pervasive and covers the gross.
- Subtle is more permanent and reliable than gross.
- Subtler has greater power than gross.
- Subtle is the cause and gross is the effect.

### Examples (Subtle To Gross)

- Vapor, water and ice cube.
- Causal body, astral body and gross body.
- Consciousness, mind and body.
- Expressions by vibrations (aura), speech and body language.
- Pleasure of bliss of consciousness, happiness of mind, pleasure of senses and illusion of pleasure of possessions.
- Morality practice in spirit, in the mind, in the speech or in action.
- Spiritual evolution, mental evolution and physical evolution.
- Accomplishment of spiritual wealth, mental and cultural wealth and material wealth.
- Fame; one is remembered in history for many generations, one is known by many people during a given lifetime. One

is famous only briefly or among a relatively small group of people.

## GUNAS (THREE QUALITIES OF NATURE)

Entire universe is created by interplay of three qualities of nature called Gunas. Gunas also sustain the universe. They are Tamas (Inertia or ignorance), Rajas (Energy or activities) and Satva (Goodness or equilibrium). On a grand scale, Brahma is the creator, Vishnu is the sustainer and Mahesh is the transformer. These are mythological figures.

At microscopic level, an atom is sustained by protons, electrons and neutrons. Proton is positive energy, electron is negative energy and neutron is neutral energy. Good and evil support and balance each other. Everything is combination of three Gunas with one Guna predominating. Total utopia of goodness is not possible. Good and evil forces help souls to evolve. Taoism uses the term yin and yang, the negative and positive forces that balance entire universe.

There are three kinds of foods, three kinds of austerities, three kinds of charities and three kinds of personalities. Our personality is combination of three Gunas with one Guna dominating the other two. Our physical constitution is combination of three Gunas. The science of Ayurveda (a secondary Veda), prescribes herbal treatment and diets based on person's body constitution. One evolves from inertia (Tamas) to activity (Raja) and reaches balance (Satva). Satva is the state of evolution necessary for awakening.

In the flow of life, beginning and end meet. Inertia (Tamas) and balance (Satva) look similar externally. One is beginning the journey and other is finishing the journey. They are on opposite sides of the spectrum, just like sunrise and sunset. A child has no hair or teeth and very old person looses hair and teeth. A prisoner suffers isolation in prison and a monk chooses isolation. A fool remains quiet due to ignorance, while a wise person remains silent because he feels futility of speech. A person in deep sleep and Samadhi look motionless on the surface; one is disconnected from consciousness while the other is connected to Supreme Consciousness. A lazy person does not do anything while a wise person renounces activities.

Rajas is in the middle and exhibits activities. A half filled pot makes noise. Water in empty pot and full pot does not make noise. A person with borrowed knowledge or half knowledge talks a lot.

## GURU

Guru means a spiritual guide. A Guru leads his disciple from Gu (Darkness) to Ru (Light). A true Guru shows direction to reach Self within instead of making dependent disciples. A true Guru becomes a mirror for his disciple to wake him up from illusion. He breaks ego of disciple to make him humble and receptive to wisdom. He becomes available to resolve all doubts of his disciple. A true Guru teaches bitter yet beneficial truth with compassion. He does not manipulate truth to attract disciples.

One cannot look for a Guru. If you can choose a Guru, you are superior to Guru. If you choose a Guru based on popularity or your emotional needs, it will be misleading. It will be an escape by belonging instead of taking charge of your life. Masses of people choose Guru because of inner insecurity, to escape responsibilities, or in the hope that miracles or instant enlightenment will occur. Many people choose to follow a Guru as part of a large group. They have freedom to interpret the message of a Guru to suit their needs and defend their behaviors. Confronting a Guru face to face threatens their ego.

One should maintain proper distance with Guru or mentor. Their presence is like fire that burns if you go too close and does not give heat if you remain at a distance. You can read a book at a proper distance and cannot read if it is too close or too far. Proper distance means humility and respect. There are three steps to receive wisdom from a master. They are prostration, asking questions and serving. Deep essence of them is to be open to receive, ask sincere questions and follow the instructions of a master with unwavering faith.

Guru appears when a disciple is ready. One's eyes open up to recognize a Guru. The guru and disciple relationship is direct one-to-one relationship. When a student gets involved in the learning process and becomes humble, his teacher becomes his Guru without external rituals.

One cannot have an absentee Guru, dead Guru or books about a Guru. These cannot guide you personally. They can only inspire you. Only a lighted candle can light other candles.

## HELP AND SERVICE (SEVA)

Help involves ego, desire, compulsive programming or guilt. In the suffering of others, one sees one's own reflection and helps from sympathy or pity. Help involves superimposing our desires on others. People try to feed who are not hungry and preach sermons to those who are not willing to listen. People try to help others because they are told by their religion and feel guilty if they do not do voluntary work. They feel stress and spread stress because they help out of compulsion and without enough reservoir of energy. They may lack real love and understanding.

Selfless service is the product of love and compassion. One has a surplus to offer others without depleting their own resources. One offers unconditional service with love at a proper time and place to the deserving recipient. Indiscriminate service causes problems. Feed a street person who claims to be hungry and begs for money. If you give money, he may misuse it. Selfless service purifies the mind, dissolves ego and expands consciousness. One should spend retirement years meditating and providing selfless service instead of feeling worthless, holding on to possessions, worrying about health and fearing death. An older person can help others with experiences of lifetime. These can guide and inspire younger generation.

## HUMILITY (NAMRATA)

Humility means to be lower. We gain by being humble and lose by being stiff or egotistical. A valley fills up with water while mountain tops remain dry. Strong and stiff trees are snapped in a storm while flexible trees bend and survive.

Spiritual teachings flow to those who have open mind, respect for the teacher and humility. If your cup of tea is full or kept up side down, you get nothing. You can fill the container with water depending on its size. If it has holes you lose what is collected. If the container is dirty it will contaminate water. A true spiritual master breaks an ego of a disciple to make him humble and receptive instead of building his ego.

There are external gestures of humility like folding hands, lowering head, bowing down or prostration. Humility should be practiced in its spirit. One should not exhibit humility for show. One may act humble but build subtle ego.

## IMPERMANENCE (ANITYA)

Entire universe and everything within it is in a state of flux, constantly vibrating and changing at different frequencies. The exception is Self (Atman). Insects live for seconds while mountains remain for millions of years. Everything is born, exists, grows, decays and dies in time. Self remains in the background as a constant witness. Supreme Consciousness is like an ocean and all living creatures are like waves. Waves come and go while the ocean remains constant. Life is like a bubble of water which can burst at any moment. This awareness teaches us to live in the moment and live one day at a time without attachments.

Vivek means spiritual discrimination, to be able to see impermanent nature of everything which looks solid and real. With this vision once can remove attachment to things and loved ones. One removes attachment to own changing body. One renounces cravings of mind and remains as a blissful witness.

Quantum physics has proven that there is only unified field of consciousness. Entire universe is empty. Solid, liquid and gaseous matters are nothing but illusion. They are the result of vibrating electromagnetic energy at different frequencies. Vedanta calls our universe Maya (illusion).

We can find peace when we accept Self as permanent reality and world as relative reality or dream. Our body goes through aging, sickness and death. We can live with awareness and grow in wisdom with aging or attach to our impermanent possessions and body and suffer. When one is awakened, he sees the world as a temporary cosmic dream and experiences joy of being an observer.

## INFORMATION, KNOWLEDGE, WISDOM

Information is received by the mind. It is reflected upon by intellect and meditated upon by consciousness.

Information is food. Knowledge is like chewing it and digesting it. Wisdom is like energy received from the food, which is also stored in the body for future use. Wisdom is the energy that guides our life and stores the energy as Sanskaras which build our character and personality.

When one receives information it is called Sruti. One analyzes with logic and reason, it is called Yukti. When one contemplates

75

and applies in life, it is called Anubhuti.

These days we are bombarded with overload of information that has created confusion. Choose the information selectively and put into practice.

## KARMA

Karma means action. Karma is the universal law of cause and effect. Entire universe is governed by it. There are no exceptions. Laws of science such as gravity or electricity follow law of Karma.

We produce Karma with our thoughts, speech and actions. Karma caused by mind is invisible yet most powerful. Karmas are produced due to intensity of intention and feeling of doership. If one uses body, senses and mind as instrument of God, one does not produce Karma. Karma produces its results at physical, mental or emotional levels (Karma vipak). Results of Karma again become cause of other Karmas. Karmas can bring instant or delayed results. Some karma of previous lives is stored in the unconscious mind and manifest in the current life as sudden profit or loss. This is called fate or Prarabdha. We produce our own fate. Karmas leave positive or negative impression on unconscious mind (Chitta) called Sanskaras. Depth of Sanskaras depends upon attachment and intensity. Sanskaras control our life.

## LIFE IS A SCHOOL TO LEARN LESSONS

When one gets involved in life, he gets stuck. If one ignores life, he becomes escapist. One has to use positive and negative experiences of life to learn valuable lessons. One can learn lesson with small experiment instead spending entire life to learn that lesson. Sometimes one can be aware and observe the life of others and learn lessons instead of wasting time. One can utilize positive situations as blessings of God and difficult situations as challenge and an opportunity to cultivate renunciation.

When one drives at slow speed, one barely feels drizzle of rain. But seems like downpour as one increases speed. One who is evolving faster seems to face more difficulties. Lifting greater amount of weight builds stronger muscles. Same way, facing greater difficulties builds spiritual muscles of spiritual maturity.

If one is not aware, he will repeat the same mistakes until he wakes up and learns lessons. Life is a school that teaches lesson for the maturity of soul (Jivatma). One has to fulfill all desires of material life by experiencing it directly or by spiritual discrimination. One cannot suppress desires. When one gains maturity by living with awareness, attraction to the world drops away and one becomes a renunciate.

World is like high school and spiritual life is like college. One has to graduate from high school to enter the college. Material and spiritual life require the same disciplines. In both cases, one has to balance time, money and energy and sacrifice comforts to stay on the path of success. But these are in opposite direction to each other. Worldly path is dead-end. Spiritual path brings true satisfaction. One has to turn around and change the direction in life.

Spiritual success is more difficult than material success. In material life, one accumulates and builds ego while spiritual life requires renunciation and dissolution of ego. Material life requires focus on external world while spiritual life focuses on internal world. Material life requires control of external forces while spiritual life requires control of own mind. In material life, you can get help from others while in spiritual life you travel a lonely path. Material success is visible and people can complement you while spiritual success is subtle and one needs patience and inner strength to continue. The person who cannot manage material life will fail on the spiritual path. He may become escapist or a scholar but not a true practitioner. The person who knows how to succeed in material life can change the direction and apply the same disciplines to succeed in spiritual life.

## LOVE AND ATTACHMENTS (MOHA)

Love is God. Unconditional love grows and expands consciousness. It has no boundaries. Love is unconditional and is experienced in the heart. One loves without any expectations and remains peaceful. When one thinks about love and expects from others, it becomes attachment. When one tries to control any person or situation, one becomes attached and gets controlled. Attachments are like strings that bind you and drag you.

Attachment is running towards pleasure (Raga) and running away from pain (Dwesha). Love is the experience of contentment in the present. Attachment makes you a slave. Most of human suffering is produced due to attachments.

Attachments are built by repeated association. One becomes attached to material possessions, habits, food, body, senses, mind, emotions and beliefs. One builds attachments to fulfill inner insecurity. One becomes greedy and hoards. Emotional attachment to loved ones is the most difficult to remove. Conditional love becomes attachment (Moha). One considers attachments as love. One expects reciprocation from loved ones. Many problems of family feuds and generation gap are produced because of attachments. Parents want to help and control their children with their experiences in life instead of first understanding them and their needs. On the other hand, if one misunderstands non-attachment, he may practice indifference which is worse than attachment. Indifference makes one self centered and lacks sensitivity. One feels isolation and suffering. Unconditional love can be cultivated by selfless service without expectation.

We do not own any one. All the souls in this life were in different relationships in previous life. Interaction with all souls is for learning spiritual lessons. Due to Maya, we build attachments. Attachments exist at subtler level. Premature renunciation takes perverted form. One finds replacement. Some people become monks and renounce world for spiritual practices. He renounces home but builds or depends on Ashrams and gets attached. He renounces family and becomes a Guru and gets attached to his disciples. One becomes proud of renunciation and exhibits it for recognition, fame or power. One can cultivate renunciation gradually with awareness and spiritual discrimination. Permanent renunciation (Param vairagya) takes place only after experiencing Self (Atman) and rising above three Gunas of nature.

Love is the experience of heart while attachment is the product of mind. When one is in the mind, love disappears and when one is in love, mind disappears. Love keeps you in the present while attachments take you in the past and future.

## MACROCOSM AND MICROCOSM
## (BRAHMAND AND PIND)

Entire universe involves the interplay of five microscopic rudimentary elements (Panch maha bhutas). This interplay is the result of the three forces (Gunas) of nature (Prakriti). Five basic elements are earth, water, fire, air and space. Three forces are Tamas (ignorance or lethargy), Rajas (Activity) and Satva (Purity and balance).

At a grand scale, planet with oceans and continents, and entire universe is called Macrocosm. Macrocosm is made by Brahma or creator, Vishnu or sustainer and Mahesh as destroyer. These three mythological Gods represent three main three forces of nature. Microcosm is the miniature manifestation of it as all living creatures. Five elements existing at microscopic level are protons, electrons and neutrons. Everything in the universe has built-in consciousness and energy. Varieties of cells in human body are self-regulated. Everything in the universe that looks gross, liquid or gaseous is nothing but vibrating electromagnetic energy along with consciousness.

Universe is contained within universe. At miniature scale, human body is called Microcosm. Our body's constitution is similar to the earth containing mostly water. Within our body there are further miniature universes. Feet represent the map of entire body. It is called reflexology. Eyes represent the map of entire body, and it is called iridology.

If you study a single crystal of salt, you know the chemistry of all salts of the universe regardless their origin is ocean or mountain. By knowing the mystery of human body, mystery of the universe can be known.

## MASTER OR SLAVE

A master controls and a slave is controlled. We have a choice in life to be a master or a slave. The choice is made by the intellect. Restless and scattered mind along with indecisive and impure intellect makes us slave while pure intellect makes us a master.

With technological advancement, we should have more time and more comfort. But most people complain they lack time and peace of mind.

1. They possess more than they need and have to spend more time to earn money to pay for it. Those who borrow money and have to pay interest or penalty are slaves.

2. Some depend on gadgets of technology and become addicted to them. People become addicted to video games, computers, face book or e-mails. They waste time and lose capacity to think or be

creative. This is slavery.

3. Indiscriminate use of gadgets produces slavery. Text messaging and e-mails are useful to reach someone in meeting. But if you use it to avoid direct contact, it wastes more time. A phone call can resolve issue directly.

4. Being addicted to Facebook, YouTube or news wastes time. One gets into arguments or gossiping and wastes energy.

5. By being preoccupied with gadgets people lose direct human contact and communication. Family members miss bonding with love.

The guideline is to use the products that give you more benefits than slavery and use wisely instead of being a victim.

## MAYA

Maya means cosmic illusion. Everything we perceive through senses and mind is called Maya. Maya is considered cosmic illusion because it constantly changes with time (Kala), place (Desh) and circumstances (Paristhiti). Due to Maya, we perceive all names and forms and dualities of you and I. Atman is constant reality that observes changing world without getting involved.

Atman/Brahman is constant reality that supports Maya. Maya is the projection on the screen of Brahman. Brahman is eternal reality while Maya is relative reality. Brahman is like cosmic ocean of energy and all living creatures are like waves. All waves are part of the ocean. Ocean can exist without waves but waves cannot exist without ocean. Due to Maya one sees own self as individual wave and forgets basic nature is Infinite Ocean.

All the objects and beings in the world are considered Maya because they come into existence and are destroyed in time. They are not constant in all places, times or situations.

Maya is the cause of bondage but same Maya can be utilized to attain freedom. Our mind, intellect and consciousness are in Maya and can be utilized to liberate us. One can make a quantum leap and wake up from Maya.

The term Maya is used in Vedanta philosophy is similar to term Prakriti is used in Sankhya philosophy.

## MIND AND BODY CONNECTION

Mind and body are one and the same. Mind is the subtle part of the body while body is the gross part of mind. Mind is the cause and body is the effect. Prana connects our gross, astral and causal bodies. Consciousness is the neutral observer in the back ground. Unconscious mind (Chitta) controls functions of our body. Traumatic experiences of life get locked in the muscles of the body. With deep massage or deep meditation one can eliminate deep scars of the mind.

Dr. John Sarno did extensive research and found that pain in the neck or back is caused by hidden deep rage in the mind. Louise Hayes mentions the root cause of many ailments of body is hidden in the mind. Some of the affirmations in this book can be utilized for communicating with unconscious mind to heal you.

One needs to heal life instead of just the body. Food and medicines heal physical body. Deeper healing takes place by utilizing prana and the mind (Astral body). Deepest healing takes place by tuning into Consciousness (Causal body).

## MODERATION

Moderation is natural middle path. Moderation in sleeping, eating and recreation is ideal for meditation and ideal for health. Indulgence produces guilt and guilt produces suppression. Suppression cannot be sustained. It turns into indulgence again. The cycle continues.

One has to experience both indulgence and suppression to some extent to appreciate the value of middle path.

Moderation is natural and effortless state of being. Natural state is like a rubber band. Rubber band can be stretched with force but returns to normal position when released. If we listen to our body and prana, they will lead us to moderation. Animals follow moderation because of instinct. If we pay attention to our senses and mind, they will disturb moderation.

String instruments work the best when they are tuned properly. Moderation can be produced with self love. If we love our body and mind, we will not abuse them with indulgence or suppression. Moderation is the result of integrated disciplines in life. One learns to love and accept self and flow with life. Disciplines follow effortlessly.

## NEEDS, WANTS, DESIRES

Our basic necessities in life are food, shelter and clothing. These needs are the means for the spiritual goal of Self-Realization. We let our senses direct our minds which further projects desires. Desires grow and complicate life, producing slavery and misery. One should reduce wants and desires to find peace. Restless mind promotes desires while quiet mind takes one towards contentment. Wants and demands allow economy to grow and promotes research to improve quality of life. We cannot fight progress, but rather use wisely to our advantage and learn to be content. Use wisdom in making choices in life. Avoid the evils of competition, stress, and quarrels produced by new technology and social media.

## PAIN AND SUFFERING (DUKKHA)

Life is painful from birth until death. This pain is due to bondage of time and space. Birth, death and transmigration are considered painful process. Pain is integral part of life. It is unavoidable. Pain is a sensation. It is necessary for survival. It gives signal if there is any health hazard. Pleasure and pain are duality or two sides of a coin. One is hidden in the other. We are attracted to sensation which pleases us and repelled by sensation which displeases us. Pleasure and pain are relative sensations. Decreased pleasure becomes painful and decreased pain feels pleasurable. After comfort of air conditioning, fan feels painful. But during intense heat, a fan gives comfort.

Resistance to pain exaggerates pain and is called suffering. Suffering can be avoided. If we flow with the pain, suffering is reduced. Duality increases suffering. Being homogeneous reduces suffering. Flowing with life and living in the present reduce pain and suffering. Suffering is produced by thinking of the past and projecting in the future. A visit to a dentist magnifies suffering because of thinking of the past experience or worrying about the future.

Attachments increase pain and suffering. When you lose something, it produces suffering in proportion to attachment. It does not hurt us if a stranger is injured but hurts when loved one is injured.

## PATIENCE AND PERSEVERENCE

Patience and perseverance are the most required aspects for spiritual evolution. Patience means sustaining steadiness during misfortune, temptations, irritations, annoyance and restlessness. Perseverance means continuous effort and adhering to the direction in spite of difficulties, successes, failures. All obstacles can be met with a smiling face and enthusiasm.

Yogi Patanjali defines yoga and meditation as controlling thought waves and being established in the Self. Constant sustained effort to control restless mind with enthusiasm is called Abhyas (Steady practice). Removing attraction to the world is called Vairagya (Renunciation). Lord Krishna in Bhagavad Gita also recommends Abhyas and Vairagya to control the restless mind. These are the backbone of spiritual success.

Patience and perseverance were very natural when there was continual hardship for survival and scarcity of necessities of life. The greatest evil of modern technology is comforts, abundance and freedom. They have made people weak, lazy and restless. Many people are impatient, intolerant and scattered. These days, information is available on any topic instantaneously. However, very few people seem to sustain steady practice. People are attracted to new gimmicks, escapes, illusions and instant success, and run from one path to the other. They seem to be inspired, but cannot sustain enthusiasm to put into practice. Very few people seem to practice simple yoga routine, breathing, meditation or dietary disciplines on daily basis. Their practice is goal-oriented and they give up easily if they do not get instant results. They dig many shallow holes looking for water instead of finding proper spot and digging until water flows. They are programmed to follow external authorities instead of taking charge of own life.

## PEACE (SHANTI)

Everyone is looking for peace. They spend entire life in the search and find frustration. They are looking for it in the wrong direction. Peace is our basic nature and searching for it is running away from it. Exploring externally with awareness, give us maturity to change the direction inward.

Most people look for peace by gaining wealth, pleasure, fame, power or activities. Impermanent things cannot give peace. They can only entice you and bring suffering.

People use sense organs to experience peace from outside. Sense organs themselves are impermanent. Sense objects are also impermanent.

People use mind to explore peace. Mind and emotions fluctuate between past and future. They give illusion of pleasure. Mind is a small reflection of Atman and has no capacity to experience peace. Peace is experienced by realizing self effulgent Atman.

Some people and organizations try to spread peace with social movements or charitable trusts. They often create noise instead of peace. Peace can be spread only being peaceful and setting an example.

Only permanent thing is Consciousness, which is expression of Atman. Solution to find peace is to be still. Let the body, senses and mind settle down in the present. Let go of all regrets of the past and ambitions of the future. Remain content within the Self (Atman). There is nowhere to go, nothing to accomplish, nothing to do. You are perfect here and now.

Withdraw all energies from outside like electricity is turned off, and bring within Atman (Within spiritual heart), the power house and the reservoir.

## PRAKRITI

Brahman is eternal universal consciousness. It splits as consciousness or Purusha or God and energy as Prakriti or Goddess. Combination of Purusha and Prakriti creates universe. Purusha and Prakriti are eternal. Prakriti means procreation. Pra means pro and kriti means creation.

God is like a dancer and creation is his dance. This is called Leela. We are all part of God's dance. We possess divine qualities and are the co-creators of our destiny.

Entire universe is nothing but energy and vibrations manifesting as names and forms of solid, liquid or gaseous matter. Behind all living creatures there is a direct connection. We are all one as Consciousness and connected with same energy just like all waves are part of the ocean. Prana pervades entire universe and regulates it.

The term Prakriti is used in Sankhya philosophy is similar to the term Maya used in Vedanta philosophy.

## PRANA

Prana is the subtlest unit of energy that pervades entire universe. Everyone and everything is connected with Prana. Prana sustains human body. When Prana departs body, it dies. We have five major Pranas and five minor Pranas that control all functions of our body. Prana pervades our gross, astral and causal bodies and allows them to work harmoniously. Gathering prana and regulating flow of Prana in body produces health. Obstruction to flow of Prana is called disease.

Prana and Apana are major Pranas. Prana resides in the heart and represents space element which is the subtlest and controls the five sense organs. Apana resides at the anus and represents earth element which is the grossest element. It controls elimination functions.

In grosser sense, breath is Prana. Yoga practices involve breathing techniques which regulate Prana for special benefits. Yoga positions focus on vital organs and nervous system for proper flow of Prana instead of focusing on building muscles. During advanced yoga positions, one surrenders to prana and allows it to move the body. Real yoga practices involve union of Prana and Apana to awaken spiritual power called Kundalini. In martial arts practice, advance practitioners mostly use Chi (Prana) instead of muscles.

We receive Prana through, food, sunshine, breathing and meditation. Food is the grossest means which produces waste. Breathing and meditation are subtlest and most direct sources to receive Prana. Moral conduct, selfless service and controlling sexual energy preserves energy. Refined Prana becomes aura which is its invisible manifestation. Evolved people radiate vibrations. Their speech and presence are soothing. Our presence speaks for itself with our auras more than speech and actions. Places accumulate their vibrations. People with spiritual vibrations can heal others by touch, speech, sight, thoughts or mere presence. Prana predominantly radiates through fingertips and toes. This is why healers use their hands and devotees touch the feet of their masters.

These days people become self-made healers, but cannot heal own self. People get certificate with one week training and commercially heal others for personal gain. They get training in mechanical practice and do not learn how to build and preserve Prana. They get exhausted when trying to heal others and feel stress.

## PRAYERS, MEDITATION AND SURRENDER
Prayers are talking to God. Meditation is listening to God. Surrender is obeying God. Prayers involve duality of a prayer as a subject and God as an object. One asks God for favors. Meditation unifies subject and object. Mind dissolves. One experiences bliss. Surrender allows one to be an instrument of God.

Most people pray to God only in the time of trouble and forget to pray during comforts of life. The cycle of pleasure and pain continues. If one prays to God during the pleasures of life, the cycle of suffering will end. God answers all sincere prayers. What we pray for may not be wise, pleasing only for a while, or may bind us eventually. Praying out of gratitude and asking for nothing becomes meditation. In meditation God provides what is good for us.

Many ancient prayers are directed towards health, happiness and peace in the world. Prayers have no boundaries of space. Praying for others sends healing vibrations and also heals us. Group prayers and synchronized prayers have power to heal others.

## PROCRASTINATION (PRAMAD)
Procrastination is the greatest hindrance to material or spiritual success. One procrastinates due to illusion that "I have many years to life." Live like you have limited time and set priorities to avoid procrastination. One should practice evaluation and introspection on regular basis and set priorities and urgency. One can keep a diary to set daily goal, monthly goal, yearly goal and goal of life as direction.

Other extreme of procrastination is over active mind that thinks too much instead of acting. Some people look at long term goal and become anxious for results. One should keep goal as direction and pay attention to each moment and live one day at a time. Procrastination becomes a habit. It reflects behavior such as being late at appointment, late in paying bills or missing a plane ride. Procrastination habit can be broken with awareness and working with a simple task one at a time. Sustained effort removes habits.

## PURITY (SHAUCH)

One needs to purify physical body, mind, emotions and intellect. These are means for meditation.

One needs to purify intellect. Intellect is the decision-making part of the mind. Purified intellect gives direction for liberation. Impure intellect is subject to temptation and leads towards bondage. One should purify the mind (Intellect) and emotions by cleansing it from six vices. Desires, anger, greed, ego, attachments and hatred are considered six enemies. Slowing down restless mind with relaxation and meditation helps in purification of the mind.

One needs to purify internal body by proper diet, six yogic practices (Shad kriyas) or five Ayurvedic practices (Panch karma). One needs to purify external body with bathing. Bathing in holy rivers is an external means for purifying the mind.

You can purify your body and mind considering them as a temple to invite God. This will make purification process effortless.

## PURUSHARTHA (ATTAINMENTS)

There are four attainments possible during human life: Wealth (Artha), pleasure (Kama), moral living (Dharma), and liberation (Moksha).

Most people waste their lives unconsciously running after wealth and pleasures. Wise people are willing to sacrifice wealth and pleasure for Dharma and Moksha. Wealth and pleasure are temporary attainments and give short lasting happiness that is destroyed at death. Moral living and efforts for liberation give us peace in the present life and survive death.

World is a school to experience life. We cannot suppress desires of wealth and pleasures. Use them as a means instead of goal. Remain as an observer and allow them to flow. Do not be over-excited by pleasure or depressed by pain. They pass away in time. Remain calm like an ocean that remains unperturbed during floods and droughts.

Dharma is living in rhythm with nature. It maintains our physical and mental health. Performing our duty without expectations minimizes effects of Karma. Effect of Karma continues in the next life.

Moksha is the undercurrent that directs our life. Awareness and desire for liberation takes us in the direction of Self-Realization. It survives death and allows the soul to continue the journey in the next life.

## RENUNCIATION (SANYAS)

Renunciation means willingly giving up something you love. In spiritual life, renunciation means giving up the attachment to the world. There is a tug of war between the world and spiritual life. Worldly attractions usually refer to the pleasures of the senses, material possessions, comforts, fame and power. These attractions prevent us from exploring the Self.

Ancient Vedic traditions established four stages of life (Ashrams): student life, householder's life, semi-retired life and renunciation. Renunciation is the last quarter of life to retire from the world and dedicate time for meditation and selfless service. Buddhist tradition encouraged the system 2500 years ago. One renounces the world and becomes a monk at an early age in search for God. Monks remain celibate, give up worldly possessions and make living by begging. Society and government support them. The tradition got contaminated and people became monks to escape responsibilities of life.

Yogi Patanjali describes renunciation as removing attraction and cravings to the objects of the world in the present and removing desires for them in the future. This is considered primary renunciation. One attains supreme renunciation (Param Vairagya) after one experiences the Self (Atman) directly and transcends the three modes of nature (Prakriti). Supreme renunciation leads to liberation.

For practical purpose, one does not need to give up anything. One should cultivate non-attachment gradually with awareness. If one gives up attachments prematurely or suppresses desires, these will merely grow with more intensity. It is like pruning a plant helps more growth. One should cut out the roots of attachments.

One can perform own duty and let go of attachments to results. As one evolves, he lets go of worldly ambitions, surrenders results to God and remains content with what comes naturally. One focuses on meditation and service. This renunciation comes as a result of spiritual discrimination (Vivek). One can renounce the world at any age when one has lived in the world fully and has no attraction left for it. One does not give up anything with force but drops away attachments with spiritual wisdom. Renunciation brings lasting peace.

## REPENTANCE (PRATIKRAMAN)
Repentance means recalling mistakes made during the day by thoughts, words or deeds that produce disturbance or guilt. Daily repentance removes Sanskaras in earlier stages before they get rooted in the unconscious mind (Chitta). Repentance is sincere confession in the presence of God with an open heart to remove the roots of all conflicts. Repentance connects one with deep unconscious mind and makes impact in life and transforms life. One forgives others and oneself and resolves not to repeat the same mistake again. Superficial mechanical religious confession is only an escape.

## RETIREMENT (NIVRUTTI)
Retirement period is the golden years of life. You should reap the fruits of your entire life's work. Retirement is like going from explosion to implosion and is shocking. It is like you are travelling at 100 mile per hour speed and have to stop suddenly. Many people get sick and die prematurely because they have nothing to look forward to. They feel useless. Many people work until they die because they are afraid that they will die if they stop working. The problem is that people become workaholics, slaves to work. They lose capacity to enjoy life.

The solution is to start partial retirement many years before retirement and cultivate creative hobbies. Save enough money to earn independence at retirement. Prepare mentally.

Retirement is the last stage of life to renounce world and to mediate and serve unconditionally. There are many areas where one can serve and find real fulfillment. Older persons can serve younger generation. They have experiences of life and wisdom, while young people have energy but need direction and guidance. Sharing and serving give joy and take away loneliness.

## SAMATA
Samata means balance and mental equilibrium. One should not get

highs and lows due to pleasure/pain, gain/loss, and honor/insult dualities. It disturbs our peace and drains our energy. Maintain equilibrium by being an observer. Remain at the center like a center of a wheel that remains constant while everything on the circumference moves. Our real Self is always quiet when turmoil surrounds us, just like eye of hurricane remains quiet. Consciousness remains like an observer of all ups and downs. Bhagavad Gita calls this a Sthitapragna State. Samata is necessary for meditation and tranquility of mind.

When climax of Samata is attained, one transcends three Gunas of nature. Friends and foes, gold and mud look alike to him. The external state of a fool and enlightened master may look alike.

## SANSKAR

Essence of all pleasant and unpleasant experiences register in the unconscious mind (Chitta) and are called Sanskaras. Unconscious mind is like invisible part of an iceberg. We are constantly bombarded by media messages. Relaxed mind absorbs Sanskaras most effectively. We pick up maximum Sanskaras in mother's womb, and then age 7 to 12. After that we function at beta wave frequency and remain less receptive. Repeated thoughts and actions hardwired in the brain become Sanskaras.

Depth of Sanskara is in proportion to intensity of attachment. Strong likes and dislikes register as Sanskaras. If we live with awareness and serve unconditionally as instrument, we do not register as Sanskaras. Shallow Sanskaras are like a line drawn on sand and deeper Sanskars are like etching on a rock. They are like undercurrent and control our life more than forced disciplines and intellectual information. Our habits and addictions are results of our Sanskaras. Repetitions deepen Sanskaras. Sanskaras of many lifetimes become our personality (Swabhav). Sanskaras can be changed by communicating with our unconscious mind with awareness or deep meditation. Use the affirmations in this book for reprogramming the mind.

Regression to past experience with deep meditative awareness can remove Sanskaras. One can get in habit of writing a diary and writing it as thoughts and emotions flow spontaneously. It gets us in touch with unconscious mind and releases deep impressions. Deep repentance, spontaneous dancing, singing and praying with deep emotions, and uninhibited laughing are other means for releasing deep tensions.

## SATSANG

Sat means truth, God or Self. Sang means association. Any association that inspires you to connect with higher Self is Satsang. Everyone needs guidance, support and enthusiasm to sustain practice.

Without Satsang, our practices become mechanical and boring. When a group gathers for the same purpose, there is collective energy. In forest fire green trees burn easily.

What we cannot attain by forced disciplines or intellectual lectures can be easily attained by Satsang. Satsang cleanses impurities of the mind and awakens deep rooted spiritual feelings and brings on the surface. Our unconscious mind is filled with positive and negative sanskaras, just like good plants and weeds in the garden. Satsang nurtures good sanskaras and destroys bad sanskaras.

Our daily practice and contemplation, and reading scriptures and affirmations become means of Satsang. Environments support our practice. One should arrange meditation room in the house for the meditation purpose only. Decorate it with flowers and pictures of saints, mentor or deity. Remove all furniture. Meditate there regularly to build vibrations. It will provide calming feeling by entering the room.

If you cannot get chance for Satsang, avoid the negative associations called Kusang. Avoid the people and situations that distract you from the path.

## SECLUSION (EKANT)

Seclusion is generally understood as isolation, being alone in privacy without company of others. Prisoners are kept in seclusion and deprived of human contact as punishment.

For spiritual purpose, one chooses seclusion for peace, revival and meditation. During seclusion, one gets chance to work with own self without external distractions. One chooses a mountain, woods, river, shore or cave away from people. Spiritual buildings such as monasteries can also provide silence and seclusion.

Seclusion provides environment suitable for focusing within.

During seclusion, one gives up comforts and distractions of senses but carries own mind with him. One cannot run away from his own mind but can transcend mind. Some people use seclusion as an escape. One can get used to seclusion and can get disturbed by returning to normal life.

True essence of seclusion is to be alone with your true Self. One realizes by experiences in the world that there is no savior outside. One gives up dependence on external authorities and realizes that there is nowhere to go but be still and experience. One does not run away from reality of life. One can perform all duties without attachments. One simplifies life, reduces social activities, moderates food, sleep and activities and gives up stimulations of senses. One practices evaluation, introspection, meditation and affirmations on regular basis and reads scriptures for inspiration. One can maintain awareness during active day and cultivate spiritual discrimination and renunciation during experiences of life. One maintains Satang with like minded people or own mentor.

## SEEKERS (SADHAK)
There are four kinds of seekers: those seeking relief from suffering (Aartra), those seeking wealth and pleasure (Artharthi), the curious (Jignasu) and those seeking wisdom (Gnani). Seekers of spiritual wisdom are the true seekers. Wise seekers pray to God out of gratitude and want nothing. God provides everything without asking.

Out of thousands there is only one true seeker who is willing to sacrifice everything for the search of Self. Most people search for God to help them escape or experience pleasures of the external world.

The greatest human suffering is transmigration. Birth and death cycle is ultimate bondage. True spiritual search is search for liberation from transmigration.

## SELF LOVE
Self love is the starting point to improve our life or to break away from destructive behaviors. One unconsciously punishes own self by indulging in harmful physical and mental activities. Harsh disciplines or suppressions do not last. One has to accept and love one's own self.

Law of Karma means all actions bring results. The impression of action also registers in the unconscious mind. All the experiences of the past, the feeling of sin or guilt, real or imagined manifest in the later years of life. Childhood abuses of physical or mental nature leaves scars in the unconscious mind. They result as self-punishment and self-created suffering.

This behavior can be eliminated by affirmations during relaxed state of mind. Practice repentance and forgive others who offended you in the past and also forgive yourself. Surrender to the forgiving God within. Focus deep within the spiritual heart and feel divine spark of God within. Allow God's radiant light to spread through your entire being. Let it remove the darkness of ignorance, anger and hate and saturate it with love and compassion. Experience the deep impurities burning to ashes. Let the radiant light spread beyond the boundaries of your body.

## SHORTSIGHTED OR VISIONARY

If you rely on your senses, impulses and temptations of mind, you become short-sighted. You speak and react without thinking. If you are a visionary, you think first and evaluate the situation with a long-term outlook before speaking or acting. You rely on your intellect and use spiritual discrimination (Vivek) to make proper choices and set priorities. You can quiet the mind by observing the breath until it becomes rhythmic, and remaining as an observer.

If you are short-sighted you become blind. You see part of life and make wrong choices. You speak and act impulsively and regret later on. You miss the essence of life. You get attracted to temporary pleasures and sacrifice permanent bliss.

If you become a visionary, you make proper choices. You act constructively and make temporary sacrifices for long-term happiness.

Politicians and spiritual leaders are often short-sighted. For their personal greed they sacrifice ecological system and world peace. In business world, people become successful by being visionary. In social and family relations one needs to be visionary to maintain healthy relationship. At personal level also, people suffer because of being shortsighted and react impulsively to speech and actions of others. They forget long-term view of relationship. Long term spiritual perspective on life brings joy.

Do not trust wavering mind. Logical mind is shortsighted and has limitation of time. Its decisions are short-sighted. Intuitive mind is visionary and gets the panoramic view of life and transcends limitation of time. Rely on your intuition even if does not make logical sense.

## SENSE CONTROL (PRATYAHARA)

We have five sense organs to see, hear, taste, touch and smell. They are the gates to dissipation of our energy. When mind associates with senses, it drains energy. Sight and sound are the major distractions that produce stress in life. Sense withdrawal is the prerequisite for concentration. Sense withdrawal is like gathering rays of sun with a magnifying glass to produce enough heat to burn cotton.

We should use the sense organs wisely. We have two nostrils for breathing continuously. We have two eyes and two ears to gather wisdom by seeing and hearing. We have only one mouth to restrain eating and talking. We cannot stop the senses completely but can use them wisely like a tortoise. A tortoise has hard shell for protection. He uses his head and legs for getting the prey and withdraws at other times.

## SILENCE (MAUNA)

Observing silence is a spiritual discipline called Mauna. It preserves energy. It helps quiet the mind for meditation. One should assign one day of the week for silence, rest and meditation.

One should control speech. Tongue has no bones and when it slips, it causes many problems. Spoken words are like arrows, once released cannot be pulled back. True silence comes by controlling five sense organs, five motor organs and the mind.

If one talks sparingly and only as necessary, one accumulates prana and gains strength in speech. It makes deeper impact on listeners. Those who talk a lot, lose power of speech

We have two eyes to see more, two ears to hear more, two nostrils to breathe more and only one mouth to eat and talk. We should control our speech and taste (food intake).

## SIMPLICITY (AARJAV)

One should simplify life. There is greater joy and freedom in simpler life than pleasure or indulgence. Possessions possess us. We need only food, clothes and housing. We can reduce our wants, wishes and desires. It takes lots of time and energy in accumulating and maintaining objects. Attachment causes miseries when they are lost, stolen, or broken.

Simplicity can be extended to social life and activities. Do not waste time trying to impress others. Simplicity helps contentment and peace. As one evolves, focuses on Self, and reduces dependence on others, simplicity happens naturally.

## SIN AND GUILT

Sin and guilt are programming caused by religions. Religions promote punishments of hell and rewards of heaven for converting people. There is no geographic location for heaven and hell. There is nothing permanent. How can there be permanent heaven or hell? Everything is governed by law of Karma. There is reward for good Karmas and punishment for bad Karma in proportion to the cause. Reward and punishment takes place in the current life or future lives. Sin and guilt of childhood leave deep scars and disturb our adult life. The Sanskaras of childhood can regulate our adult life. But we are created in the image of God and we are divine. Consider God as a loving and forgiving father instead of a punishing father.

Vedanta philosophy uses the term ignorance instead of sins. Ignorance is not permanent and does not generate guilt.

Mistakes can be corrected. Mistakes are like clouds. They are not permanent. Making mistakes teach us lessons if we are aware. Mistakes should not be repeated. We should always pray to forgive others and forgive ourselves.

## SKILLFUL ACTIONS

Karma Yoga is considered skillful action. All actions produce Karma and Sanskaras. Skillful action is not limited to skill in our profession, but to actions that do not bind us to consequences. A skillful thief can rob or steal without being caught. His skill is superficial because he gets bound by his evil deed. Efficient businessman can be skillful in making money, but using immoral means brings suffering. Skillful action enables one to be successful using moral means and without attachment to results. Sharing selflessly with others can help free us from bondage to karma.

When one acts with efficiency and clarity as an instrument of God and serves without any selfish motive, one becomes free from the consequences of action. Root cause of Karma is mind and desires and the feeling that I am the doer. Remember that we are not the doers, owners or enjoyers, but only instrument of God to serve selflessly.

## SPEECH

Speech carries greater power when it is based upon truth and is filled with compassion. It makes greater impact than long intellectual lecture. One should practice truth in thought, speech and action. It produces fearlessness. If one lies one time, it takes many lies to cover it up and disturbs peace.

Speech can be soothing and compassionate and can be like a needle to mend the lives of people. Or it can be harsh and bitter and can be like a scissor to destroy life of others.

Those who know the truth, express it with a few words or in silence. Those who have borrowed information, write a lot, talk a lot or become a scholar to convince own self and others. Great seers wrote straight forward short Sutras (Statements with deep meaning) to express their personal experiences. It is said: "Those who know the Self do not talk about it. Those who talk about it do not know the Self".

It is rare to find people who teach bitter but beneficial truth with compassion because it does not make them popular. It is rare to find people who are willing to listen to the truth because they have to give up their ego and attachments.

## SUFFERING

When one evolves, one realizes that life is suffering from birth to death and all pleasures are root cause of pain. He gives up attachments to the world and focuses on permanent imperishable Self. There are three kinds of sufferings: physical (Aadhi bhautik), environmental or natural disasters (Aadhi daivik), and psychological (Aadhyatmik). We have no control over external nature. We have some control over our body. We can have greater control over our mind. We have to recognize these sufferings and utilize life as means for spiritual purpose.

Suffering comes from attachments and resistance. It is reduced by learning to flow with life and living in the present.

Many ancient prayers end with the prayer for peace. It is "Aum shanti, shanti, shanti " Shanti means peace. It is chanted three times for attaining peace.

## SURRENDER (ISWAR PRANIDHAN)

Surrender is not defeat but attunement. Surrender means letting go of resistance that drains energy. By surrendering, we merge and become homogeneous. By surrendering to God, we absorb divine qualities and become Godlike.

Prayer is talking to God. Meditation is listening to God. Surrender is obeying God. We surrender to an unknown pilot while flying, we surrender to a doctor in surgery or while taking drugs. Why not trust almighty who has created us, sustains us, and surrounds us at all times? A dog walking under a horse cart feels the burden of the cart due to ignorance. When he realizes it, he feels freedom. Due to ignorance we carry burdens of the world. When we awaken, we realize that supreme power with cosmic intelligence takes care of the entire universe. Our breathing, heart beats, digestion of food and healing goes on without our effort and laws of Karma governs entire universe.

When sailing a boat, using wind, waves and current properly is surrender. While practicing yoga positions, allowing prana to guide movements of body is surrender. Deep relaxation and allowing prana to heal is surrender.

## SWA-DHARMA

Swa-Dharma is personal duty. It liberates. Our duty changes with age, time and situation. Performing our duty guided by intuition can liberate us. If we practice Swa-Dharma, we do not need to worry about public opinion or other spiritual teachings or moral codes. Our Swa-Dharma is to please the Lord at all times.

Well performed personal duty will give liberation even if duty is common or plain. Grass looks greener at a distance. One wants to be in the shoes of others. If your duty is to clean streets, doing the job well will be more virtuous than trying to be a spiritual leader.

Emotional involvement and attachment to results can hinder

duty and disturb peace. One should not get emotionally attached doing duty as parents, children or teachers but rather serve selflessly.

## SYNCHRONICITY

Synchronicity gathers and coordinates energy. A single stick can be broken easily but becomes unbreakable in a bunch. Our energy gets wasted by scattered senses and mind and creates conflicts between mind and emotions.

As one evolves, he becomes focused and preserves energy. It results in synchronicity of thoughts, speech and action. His thoughts are synchronized with emotions. Sense withdrawal (Pratyahara) gathers energy like a magnifying glass gathers energy of sunlight. Concentration accumulates energy and meditation directs energy towards the Self (Atman). When electricity goes out, it goes to the powerhouse. Atman is the power house of life.

## TRANSMIGRATION

Transmigration means continuation. Nothing is created and nothing is destroyed. Everything changes forms. Transmigration refers to the journey of soul (Jivatma). When Consciousness identifies itself with body, senses and mind, this is called soul. Soul is in bondage due to cosmic illusion (Maya). Maya is a cosmic dream which deludes everyone.

After death, soul continues the journey in a new body to fulfill desires. It carries impression of entire life (Sanskaras). This is called reincarnation. Reincarnation is considered slavery and bondage to cycle of birth and death. Liberation means awakened state, removal of all layers of ignorance. Jivatma becomes pure Atman and free from transmigration.

## TRUTH (SATYA) AND NON-VIOLENCE (AHIMSA)

There are Ten Commandments in religions and ten rules of moral conducts in Raja yoga. Truth and non-violence are the fundamental rules. Truth is eternal and not contaminated by time, place or situations. Non-violence is the starting point of love and compassion. One has to practice truth and non-violence and other moral disciplines in the mind. This will reflect in speech and action. It will bring peace and harmony in life because it aligns our life with universal rhythm (Dharma). By practicing truth in true spirit, one's words materialize reality. Practicing non-violence in true spirit spreads feeling of non-violence to all creatures around him. Moral living is the foundation of spirituality and Raja Yoga. Dharma provides health and harmony to individuals and society.

External mechanical disciplines or literal practice of morality can harm others and own self, and will be hypocrisy. External disciplines cannot be sustained. If one restrains senses but entertains subtle pleasure in the mind, this will lead to action anyway. People join pro-life movement but use violence and disturb peace in protests. People become vegetarian to practice non-violence but hurt others with bitter speech. People practice non-stealing but cheat others in business. People practice non-violence as an escape instead of performing their duty (Dharma) to protect own family or nation against unjust aggression. People torture their body, senses and mind in name of morality instead making friendship with them to find joy. People who practice literal truth without consideration of time and place can harm others. Sometimes a white lie can spread peace and can be more in line with Dharma than literal truth.

## VARIOUS WAYS TO PERCEIVE GOD

God can be perceived as Brahman or Atman, without quality or form. Everyone and everything is Brahman. Vedanta teaches So Hum or Thou are that. Gnana yoga, Buddhism and quantum physics envision ultimate reality like Vedanta philosophy.

God can be perceived as Ishwar (According to Vedanta philosophy) or Purusha (according to Sankhya philosophy), who has quality but no form. Many religions believe in invisible God in heaven and humans as subjects. Purusha projects energy called Prakriti and is called Goddess. One can worship God to attain liberation. One can use Goddess (Prakriti) as a means to attain God (Purusha).

Hindus believe in incarnation of God as an avatar or Bhagawan. God comes down to human form in each age (Yuga), to serve his creation, to restore Dharma and liberate worthy souls. Avatar takes human form, so that one can worship God with quality and form. Bhagawan has six divine qualities (Bhagas). They are: lordship, strength, beauty, wealth, wisdom and dispassion. By worshipping and surrendering to personal God, one inherits these divine qualities and finds liberation.

There are many demigods and goddesses with special powers of God. People worship them to receive special favors.

When human beings evolve and tune into God consciousness, they become messiah or messengers of God.

There are saints, holy men and Gurus in each age, nation and culture who have spark of God and serve humanity. They do not belong to any religion and do not preach any dogma.

## VEDANTA AND QUANTUM PHYSICS

Vedanta studied universe from subjective viewpoint and found ways to find liberation. Science studied the universe from objective standpoint and found technology and comforts at the cost of inner peace. Quantum physics has validated the teachings of Vedanta. One does not need to believe the teachings by faith any more. It is the reality.

Vedanta teaches that Brahman is eternal. World is projected on Brahman and is cosmic illusion (Impermanent Maya), It goes through cycle of creation, sustenance and is destroyed at Maha Pralay. Quantum physics validates that universe is created at big bang and will be pulled into a black hole in the future.

Vedanta teaches Brahman is real and world is illusion. Names and forms are illusion. Quantum physics has proven that there is only unified field of consciousness and everything else that looks solid, liquid or gaseous is nothing but vibrating electromagnetic energy.

Vedanta teaches that Brahman is one, but due to Maya looks like many. Quantum physics says everyone and everything is interconnected. Due to names and forms it looks like many.

Vedanta taught about Akashik records that holds all memories. Quantum physics says that there is limitless field that holds all memories since big bang.

One can practice Samyam (Concentration, meditation and Samadhi) on any object and gain direct knowledge about that subject. These are called Siddhis or supernatural powers. Quantum physics says that one can get tangled with any object and can become identical.

Vedanta teaches we are all part of Brahman and after realizing it, we become liberated. Quantum physics says that entire universe is waves and energy of infinite possibilities. We are the co-creator of our destiny. We are all like waves and are part of the cosmic ocean.

## VIPASHYANA (VIPASSANA IN PALI LANGUAGE)

Vi means special and Pashya means seeing. Vipashyana means insight or mindfulness. One purifies intellect with meditation. Pure intellect along with consciousness produces awareness that transforms life. With awareness, one sees reality as it is instead of its names and forms. One sees everything as nothing but vibration and cosmic illusion. One sees Self is immutable reality. One sees own body as nothing but interplay of five basic subtle elements of earth, water, fire air and space (Panch maha bhutas). One wakes up from illusions of Maya.

Vipashyana practice involves purifying and sharpening the mind by observing breath. With purified mind and consciousness one scans own body and experiences reality first hand. It removes deep-rooted sanskaras to attain liberation. Sanskaras are released through mind in the form of visions and through the body as sensations of five basic elements.

## VIVEK

Vivek means spiritual discrimination. Vivek removes Avidya (ignorance). One clearly sees impermanence of his existence, pain behind pleasure, nature of impurities and of non-self. When you see impermanence of worldly possessions and pursuits, attraction for them drops. If you are sitting at a restaurant, eager to eat and hear the news that food is contaminated, you do not need discipline not to eat. A starving person sees a fruit basket in darkness. With light he sees the fruits are made of plastic and does not eat. Vivek represents the light of knowledge. This clear knowledge is called Vivek. Vivek can be cultivated by purifying intellect with meditation and spiritual austerities. Vivek produces non-attachment (Vairagya) effortlessly. Renunciation brings lasting peace.

## WE ARE ONE

Vedic seers declared with personal experience that we are one.

Names and forms are illusion. We have to believe by faith or learn by personal experience. Buddha, Mahavir, Christ, Mohammad and other masters and saints showed us direction to Dharma, love and compassion for all living creatures.

World has evolved exponentially. Six hundred years ago, people lived in different countries in isolation. We did not know that earth was round and revolved the sun. Today, world has become a smaller place. We are interconnected in culture and economics. We have to think globally for our well-being.

Quantum physics has proven that there is only one unified field of consciousness and everything else is empty space. Gross matter, liquids and gases appear real but are nothing vibrating electromagnetic energy. Scientific experiment in 1997 showed that when photon was split and kept 14 miles apart, still both showed same behavior. Everything in the world is interconnected. If it was connected once, it remains connected for ever. We existed at big bang and still are connected. Cosmic space retains memory of everyone who existed in the past. This is called cosmic memory bank (Aakashik records).

Everyone shares the same air, water and food. Similar blood runs through the arteries of all creatures. Everyone and everything comes from the dust and returns to dust. Creating boundaries only isolates our consciousness.

We have created boundaries of nations, but nature, animals and weather do not recognize these boundaries. We have created races, but science has shown that origin of all races was the same. We have created boundaries of religions that did not exist 5000 years ago. Universe is like a cosmic ocean and all living creatures are like waves. All waves are part of the ocean. If we identify ourselves as waves and forget our real identify as the ocean, we suffer. Waves that form and break still remain as ocean. We have to expand our consciousness and realize the unity of life and follow Dharma. With all the backing of spiritual and scientific knowledge, humanity is going against the laws of nature. Suffering is due to shrinking consciousness and making divisions of nation, race, religion and personal ego. We have to think collectively for personal evolution and salvation. We should pray for world peace and peace of the universe.

## WISDOM (GNANA)

Wisdom means ability to think and act utilizing knowledge, experience, understanding, common sense, and insight. Wisdom guides our life in proper direction with panoramic view of life.

Generally one grows in wisdom with aging. Degree of wisdom depends upon one's openness and awareness. People with awareness grow in wisdom as they grow older and find greater happiness. People without awareness feel insecurity and fear diseases and death as they grow older. They become attached to things and people and suffer.

Intellect is the judgmental faculty of mind. Purified intellect makes one wise. Logic gives us limited wisdom based upon our limited experiences of the past. It can be influenced by desires and fears. Greatest wisdom comes from intuition. Intuition transcends the mind and connects one with the Self which transcends boundaries of time.

Wisdom gives us true knowledge of Self (Vidya), which removes darkness of ignorance to find liberation. Wisdom provides us with the power for spiritual discrimination (Vivek). We gain insight to see pain behind pleasure, impermanent and impure nature of things. With insight, attraction to the world drops away effortlessly and one cultivates renunciation effortlessly. Renunciation is necessary for spiritual awakening. Renunciation brings lasting peace.

## YOGA

The word Yoga is derived from the root" Yuj" or union. Yoga means union of individual with supreme consciousness. We are created by God and separated from God due to Maya. Goal of yoga is to remove cosmic illusion of Maya and to realize Self.

Yoga also means integration of body, mind and spirit. One can use any of the following major paths or combination of paths which suits one's temperament and tendency. There are four kinds of people in the world. They are mind-oriented, heart-oriented, active and contemplative.

1. Path of knowledge (Gnana Yoga). One inquires about the nature of existence "Who am I?" with purified intellect.
2. Path of love and devotion (Bhakti Yoga). One worships

God.

3.  Path of Selfless service (Karma Yoga). One serves humanity.
4.  Royal path (Raja Yoga). One controls body and mind using eight systematic steps to find union with Self.

We use our thoughts, emotions, activities and contemplation in life. All these faculties can be utilized in practice of Yoga. Yoga is the practice to change direction in life from the world to the Self. One gets mastery of life and becomes master of own life.

## YUGA

Everything in the universe follows cyclic order, which repeats itself. Day and night is a smaller time cycle, while yearly seasons are a larger cycle. At a larger scale yet there is cycle of planets coming into existence and disappearing. At universal scale, universe is created, sustained and eventually it is destroyed over millions of years. Brahma is the creator, Vishnu is the sustainer and Mahesh is the transformer of life. These are mythological Gods. This large cycle is called MahaYuga cycle. These cycles are repeated constantly while underlying Supreme Consciousness (Brahman) remains untouched. Quantum physics believes that universe began at the big bang and will eventually be pulled into a black hole.

According to the scriptures, we are currently in Kali Yuga (Spiritual darkness) cycle. This is the end of our physical world and new cycle of Satya Yuga (Golden age) will begin. The signs of Kali Yuga are exponential changes and declined morality at individual and collective levels. We have population explosion, weapons of mass destruction, computer technology, disturbed and unstable people, drastic change in environments, and rapid means of communication. Their combinations make massive destruction possible. However, on the positive side, one can spiritually evolve at the fastest speed during Kali Yuga.

## ZERO AND INFINITY

Entire universe is created by three modes of nature (Gunas). It comes out of nothing and eventually dissolves into nothing. Existence in-between is called Jagat or Maya. Maya is cosmic illusion because it has no form and changes constantly. Universe is created and destroyed but consciousness (Brahman) remains untouched.

Consciousness is eternal. Consciousness in the potential form is called zero (Sunyata) and manifest form is called infinity (Brahman). Both are same because there is no mind, time, or space to compare. Consciousness is like a movie screen and world is projected on it. Movie is visible due to darkness of ignorance (Avidya) and disappears with the light of knowledge (Vidya). The screen remains untouched.

- Buddhism: Consciousness is non-self because all five aggregates (Skandhas) of perceptions are without substance. They are: 1. Roopa (form). 2. Vedana (feelings) 3. Sangna (sensation).4. Sanskar (habits). 5. Vignana (attitude). They call it void, sunyata or zero. Sunyata is the goal to attain freedom from transmigration. It can be attained by dissolution of ego.
- Vedanta: Expansion of consciousness, where there is nothing but consciousness. This can be attained by expansion of ego. One who expands to infinity (Brahman) is liberated. The basic mantra is "Thou art that".
- Quantum physics: Entire universe is nothing but unified field of consciousness (Infinity) and empty space (Zero) with electromagnetic energy giving illusion of visible universe. It is produced at big bang and returns to black hole.
- Meditation: World is created due to duality of you and I. Duality, Time and space are created by mind. When you drop all coverings of "I", you become zero. When you expand consciousness so that everyone and everything becomes you, you become infinite. Both are transcendental states. You experience bliss directly.

Zero = Infinity = Atman = Brahman = Self = Aum vibrations.

# OTHER PUBLICATIONS
# BY YOGI SHANTI DESAI

| | |
|---|---|
| Yoga: Holistic Practice Manual | 1976 |
| Hatha Yoga Practice Manual | 1978 |
| Meditation Practice Manual | 1981 |
| Reality Here and Now | 1996 |
| Self- I, Me, Mine, Ours, Illusions | 2002 |
| Dynamic Balanced Living | 2004 |
| Dynamic Meditation for Living | 2006 |
| Dynamic Quantum Transformation | 2007 |
| Personal to Global Transformation | 2007 |
| Wisdom for Living | 2009 |
| The Secret of Bliss | 2011 |
| Dynamic Spiritual Transformation | 2012 |
| Zero is Infinity | 2015 |
| Wake Up: Reflections for Spiritual Awakening | 2017 |
| | |
| Yoga VCR IN 1986, Converted to DVD | 2002 |
| (Complete Yoga Workout) | |

For more information visit *www.yogishantidesai.com.*

Made in the USA
Middletown, DE
06 May 2017